The Spiritual Exercises of
ST. IGNATIUS OF LOYOLA

The Spiritual Exercises of
ST. IGNATIUS OF LOYOLA

A Lived Experience

Gerald O'Collins, SJ

Paulist Press
New York / Mahwah, NJ

Cover design by Joe Gallagher
Book design by Lynn Else

Library of Congress Cataloging-in-Publication Data.
Names: O'Collins, Gerald, author.
Title: The spiritual exercises of St. Ignatius of Loyola : a lived experience / Gerald O'Collins, SJ.
Description: New York / Mahwah, NJ : Paulist Press, 2023. | Includes bibliographical references and index. | Summary: "This book presents the genesis of the Spiritual Exercises in the mid-life journey (or conversion) and experiences of St. Ignatius"— Provided by publisher.
Identifiers: LCCN 2022054556 (print) | LCCN 2022054557 (ebook) | ISBN 9780809156405 (paperback) | ISBN 9780809188031 (ebook)
Subjects: LCSH: Ignatius, of Loyola, Saint, 1491-1556. Exercitia spiritualia. | Spiritual exercises. | Spiritual life—Catholic Church.
Classification: LCC BX2179.L8 O365 2023 (print) | LCC BX2179.L8 (ebook) | DDC 248.3—dc23/eng/20230428
LC record available at https://lccn.loc.gov/2022054556
LC ebook record available at https://lccn.loc.gov/2022054557

ISBN 978-0-8091-5640-5 (paperback)
ISBN 978-0-8091-8803-1 (e-book)

Published by Paulist Press
997 Macarthur Boulevard
Mahwah, New Jersey 07430
www.paulistpress.com

Printed and bound in the
United States of America

CONTENTS

Preface..vii

1. A Midlife Journey and Experiences 1

2. Explanations, Practices, Examen, and Discernment..........10

FIRST WEEK..23

3. Principle and Foundation 25

4. Exercises of the First Week..36

SECOND WEEK 51

5. The Call of the King and the Incarnation...............................53

6. The Birth of Christ and the Shadow of the Cross...............62

7. The Life and Ministry of Christ 77

8. More from Jesus' Life, and the Elections.............................92

THIRD WEEK..103

9. The Passion and Death of Christ 105

10. The Passion and Death of Christ: Some Resources
for Prayer 112

FOURTH WEEK..123

11. The Resurrection of Jesus 125

12. The Contemplation for Attaining Love 134

Appendix I: The History and Practice of *Lectio Divina* 145

Appendix II: The Two Standards 155

Notes..159

Bibliography 175

Index of Names..179

Biblical Index...185

PREFACE

The task of reinterpreting and reappropriating classical texts and, not least, the religious classics never ends. After the Second World War (1939–45) and especially after the Second Vatican Council (1962–65), Jesuits and others promoted everywhere a richer and deeper reading of the Spiritual Exercises of St. Ignatius Loyola (ca. 1491–1556) and more authentic ways of doing retreats. This practice recovered his advice to allow "the Creator to work directly with the creature and the creature with the Creator and Lord" (SpEx 15). It was also an effective response to the call to holiness, which Vatican II recognized as reaching all the baptized (*Lumen Gentium*, the Dogmatic Constitution on the Church, 39–42).

In Asia, Australia, the British Isles, Canada, France, Germany, Italy, Latin America, Spain, the United States and elsewhere, those were golden years in the retrieval of an effective and personal contact with God through doing the Spiritual Exercises. A glance at the bibliography included at the end of this book illustrates the work of Jesuits and others who led this retrieval. But the task of interpretation and appropriation continues. In our post-pandemic world, we need to reflect further and let the Lord improve our practice.

This book, offered above all to those who seek God through doing the Spiritual Exercises and those who direct such "exercitants," comes from years of experience and publishing. Above all in Australia, the British Isles, Italy, and the United States, I have directed "exercitants" and "retreatants"—through longer and shorter forms of the Exercises—and written numerous articles about the Exercises. In Melbourne (Australia), I was invited to lecture for two years on the Spiritual Exercises for the College of Jesuit Spirituality. With two friends I was graced by the chance of publishing a course on the Exercises given by Anthony de Mello in his Pune ashram (see bibliography).

The book does not comment on every paragraph and detail in the Exercises. It sets itself to reflect creatively on all the major themes. In doing that, it takes up Ignatius's division of a retreat of approximately thirty days into four "weeks," each lasting around seven or eight days, that culminate in the Fourth Week's contemplation of the risen Jesus.

After a prologue offered by the Principle and Foundation, the First Week seeks to experience deep repentance for sin and a total turning to God. The Second Week begins with a contemplation on the kingdom of Christ and focuses on his life. The Third Week attends to his passion and death. The Fourth Week draws food for prayer from Christ's resurrection and the Contemplation for Attaining Love.

From the start we should also clarify how Ignatius uses the terms *contemplation* and *meditation*. By *meditation* he tends to mean praying over themes such as sin and hell. Where thought characterizes meditation, *contemplation* calls on the imagination to enter into the mysteries of Christ and let prayer become more a function of the heart.

With grateful thanks, I use the English translation of the Exercises produced by Joseph Munitiz and Philip Endean and published by Penguin (see bibliography). The paragraphs within the texts will be indicated by "SpEx" followed by the relevant number. Thus Ignatius's explanation of the four "weeks" occurs in SpEx 4. I strongly encourage both those who direct and those who do the Exercises to use the Penguin translation together with this book.

In publishing this work, I am aware of attaching myself to a cohort of eminent Catholic and Anglican commentators. They have inspired my desire to share the faith journey of the Exercises, which embodies the Ignatian vision and values. After many years of involvement, I continue to experience the Exercises as a remarkably powerful means for reigniting our spiritual life and enhancing our service of others.

I offer this book in the hope that it will help many Catholics and other Christians to reset their lives by finding the light and strength conveyed regularly through the Exercises. With immense gratitude, the work is dedicated to the memory of James Walsh, SJ, the founder of *The Way*. He never failed to encourage me to reflect seriously on the best Christian spirituality and spread its message and practice.

We begin with the midlife journey and experiences that prompted Ignatius Loyola to fashion the Spiritual Exercises.

I wish to thank those who in different ways helped me in the genesis of this book: Brendan Byrne, Alan Cadwallader, Tom Casey, Sarah Cook, Steve Curtin, Alicia Deak, Philip Endean, David Holdcroft, Elizabeth Lock, Michael Loughnane, Joseph Munitiz, Michael Smith, Brendan Walsh, Jared Wicks, and Christopher Willcock, as well as Donna Crilly and others at Paulist Press.

For permission to reprint copyright material I have to thank the *Australian Biblical Review* (for the reflections on Peter's mother-in-law in chapter 7), Paulist Press (for reflections on the Two Standards in Appendix II), *The Tablet* (for the account of Ignatius's midlife journey in chapter 1 and the poem by Neville Braybrook in chapter 10), and *The Way* (for the reflections on marriage vows in chapter 3, on Christ's nativity in chapter 6, and on *Lectio Divina* in Appendix I).

With grateful thanks I use the New Revised Standard Version (NRSV) translation of the Bible. Very occasionally I render for myself into English the Greek text of the New Testament.

When proposing Gospel passages for prayer, I sometimes follow Ignatius's method of setting out brief points. But chapters 6 and 7, respectively, set out at length and in dialogue with contemporary biblical scholarship what can be gleaned spiritually from Luke's story of Christ's birth and from Mark's account of the healing of Peter's mother-in-law. Since the time of Ignatius, an academic revolution has overtaken scriptural studies, encouraging us, for instance, to read each Gospel in its own terms (the method of *Redaktionsgeschichte* or redactional/editorial studies) and not mix up the accounts of what Jesus said or did (as the

Spiritual Exercises sometimes do). Attentive reading of superb modern commentaries on Matthew (e.g., Ulrich Luz), Mark (e.g., Joel Marcus), Luke (e.g., François Bovon), and John (e.g., Brendan Byrne) illustrates how contemporary scholarship takes nothing away; it provides more rather than less material for devout contemplation.

1

A MIDLIFE JOURNEY AND EXPERIENCES

What we draw from outstanding books that have shaped the religious history of the world will be greatly enlarged by knowing something of the author's life and spiritual experiences. Hence our reflections open by placing Ignatius of Loyola with other outstanding teachers of the Christian Church who went through a spiritual journey in their middle years. Then we will focus on the particular experiences that shaped and fed into the creation of the book in question, his Spiritual Exercises, and the making of the Exercises it proposes.

THE MIDLIFE JOURNEY

Born in Loyola, a Basque town forty miles from the French border, Ignatius entered the service of the treasurer of Castile. Ten years later, he joined the duke of Najera, Emperor Charles V's viceroy for Navarre, a northern section of the kingdom of Castile. In 1520 he helped to suppress a rebellion in the city of Najera. Then in 1521, the French king tried to win back Navarre. He sent twelve thousand infantry, eight hundred horsemen, and twenty-nine pieces of artillery across the frontier. Four days later the French forces were encamped about a mile from the walls of

Pamplona. There were only about one thousand troops available to defend the city, and some of these deserted.

Ignatius himself arrived at top speed on a horse. The city itself surrendered to the French forces. Ignatius and some others made their stand in the fortress of Pamplona. They were desperately outnumbered, the fortifications were incomplete, and the French had artillery.

On May 20, 1521, a cannon ball fired by the French forces storming the fortress ricocheted off a nearby wall and shattered Ignatius's right leg. Resistance ended, and Pamplona surrendered. Ignatius was taken home in a litter to the castle of his family in Loyola. The injury put an end to his career as soldier and diplomat.

After surviving several operations and a long convalescence, Ignatius left home for seventeen years of travel that took him to Jerusalem, back to Spain, north to Paris, across the channel to London, back to Spain, and then to his final home in Rome as superior general of a new religious order, the Society of Jesus (Jesuits). Often described as the time of his religious conversion and spiritual growth, these years make up the *midlife journey* of a saint who, throughout his autobiography, calls himself "the pilgrim."

In 1978 I produced *The Second Journey* (Paulist Press), an exploration of midlife journeys. Human *history*, as I realized then and later, throws up everywhere examples of such journeys: from Abraham and Sarah to Moses, from Paul of Tarsus to Mother Teresa of Calcutta, from Dante Alighieri to Eleanor Roosevelt, from John Wesley to Jimmy Carter, from John Henry Newman to Dietrich Bonhoeffer.

Western *literature* also enshrines numerous instances of such journeys in the "middle years." Such works as Homer's *Odyssey*, Virgil's *Aeneid*, and John Bunyan's *Pilgrim's Progress* present heroes driven in midlife to leave their familiar environments, attempt new projects, and travel strange roads. This is being "in the middle way," as T. S. Eliot put it in *East Coker*. He takes us back to the picture of the midlife journey with which Dante opens the *Divine Comedy*: "In the middle of life's road, I found myself in a dark wood—the straight way ahead lost."

The image of the midlife journey derives from our literary imagination as well as from undoubted history. The real world of midlife journeys has created its make-believe counterpart, which reflects and illuminates these journeys.

Mapping the characteristic pattern of such journeys will allow readers to recognize Ignatius as a case in point. At least six factors create the basic pattern.

First, a midlife journey *happens* to people. They do not voluntarily enter it. They can be swept into it by various factors. We might classify their stories into two classes according to whether the cause is some observable phenomenon or is something inward and less obvious.

Very often the catalyst appears "negative." A traffic accident, a serious illness, the birth of a disabled child, the death or infidelity of a spouse, unexpected job loss, or disillusionment over what public success has brought them can plunge people into an unexpected crisis. Left to themselves, they would never have chosen the pain of such a situation. It simply happened to them.

The battle of Pamplona and a long convalescence initiated a midlife journey for Ignatius. A brush with death caused his world of chivalry and diplomacy to disintegrate. Without his wanting or planning it, Ignatius suffered the profound upheaval that he records in his reminiscences, and a midlife journey began. Many choices feature in the later stages of his story. But the start of the pilgrimage was thrust upon him.

Second, a midlife journey characteristically includes an *outer* component—a specific journey or a physical restlessness that keeps a person traveling in the hope that "if I relocate, I will find the solution."

The outer journey may prove a real *Odyssey* or *Aeneid*. But it may be no more than a shift from the suburbs to the city, or something a little longer like Mother Teresa's 1946 train ride out of Calcutta. Of course, it is the *inner* component that brings about a genuine midlife journey. The external traveling has only a subordinate function. All the same time, some shift in place seems to be a steady feature of authentic midlife journeys.

Wesley's voyage to Georgia, Bonhoeffer's visit to New York on the eve of the Second World War, Newman's Mediterranean tour, and Ignatius's wanderings belong here. He traveled from Loyola to the Holy Land, back to Spain, north to Paris, back again to Spain, and eventually found journey's end at the Jesuit headquarters in Rome.

Third, midlife journeys entail a crisis of *feelings*, symbolized by Dante's terror at being lost in a forest. Such a crisis may arise from a recent personal failure (Wesley and Carter), unresolved conflicts from the past (St. Paul), or fears for the future (Bonhoeffer). However it happens, a powerful crisis of feelings always seems to blaze up as one is swept into a midlife journey.

Through the months of recovery from his wounds, Ignatius experienced emotions of comfort and distress—"sad and happy thoughts," as he called them. Learning to interpret and handle these fluctuating feelings constituted a vital stage in his journey. The Rules for the Discernment of Spirits (found in the Exercises) passed on to others what Ignatius had painfully found out for himself.

The afternoon of life, according to Carl Gustav Jung, brings *"the reversal of all* the ideals and values that were cherished in the morning" (italics mine).[1] These are strong words. Whether we stress this fourth point or make it more gently, midlife journeys bring a search for new meanings, fresh values, and different goals.

The roles by which people have identified themselves no longer seem important. Old purposes fade. Values and goals that gave meaning to life lose their grip. The wounds Ignatius suffered during the battle at Pamplona healed but left an ugly protrusion of bone. He was so anxious to retain his role as an elegant officer he persuaded some surgeons to cut it away. Without a murmur he endured their primitive surgery, driven by the fear that he would lose the identity by which he had defined his existence. But then a midlife journey led Ignatius to treasure other values and find a different identity.

In the language of the Exercises, Ignatius asked himself: "What have I done for Christ? What am I doing for Christ? What ought I to do for Christ?" (SpEx 53).

Fifth, people on midlife journeys repeatedly betray a deep sense of loneliness. This loneliness should eventually turn into the aloneness of a quiet and integrated self-possession. But before that happens, they will find themselves in Dante's "dark wood." Society can make them suffer deeply. For Ignatius that began with imprisonment by the inquisition in Spain. He made his pilgrimage to the Holy Land alone.

Eventually, people who pass through a midlife journey may transform their community and even society. They may resemble Aeneas, fashioning a whole new group of people. The followers Ignatius gathered around him became the "school masters of Europe" and missionaries to the human race.

The sixth and last feature in the pattern of midlife journeys concerns their end. Ideally such journeys end quietly, with a new wisdom and a coming to oneself that releases great power. Midlife journeys typically begin dramatically: For Ignatius, a cannon ball sweeps over the ramparts of a Spanish fortress; Newman suffers a severe, near-fatal illness when traveling in Sicily without his friends; Bonhoeffer sees Hitler plunge the world into war. The endings of such journeys tends to be quiet and undramatic. Ignatius limps into Rome after seventeen years on the road. Newman heads home, sensing that he has "a work to do in England." Bonhoeffer, hanged by the Nazis at the end of World War II, reminds us that midlife journeys can also have a dramatic, even tragic, ending. His influence on the world came posthumously, especially in the 1960s when his *Letters and Papers from Prison* sold by the thousands and helped inspire the civil rights movements.

Midlife journeys terminate with the arrival of true adult wisdom. It is the wisdom of those who have regained equilibrium, stabilized, and found fresh purposes and new dreams. They come to themselves in self-discovery and final self-identification, which allows them to reach out to others and prove astonishingly productive for the world. Their midlife journeys end with new dreams in which fresh responsibilities begin. Through his Exercises and the founding of the Society of Jesus, Ignatius lived out for the benefit of others what he had experienced for himself.

Such, then, are six characteristics of midlife journeys, exemplified by the story of Ignatius. Eliot's *Little Gidding* interprets such journeys as Odysseys that eventually bring us home to the place where we started: "We shall not cease from exploration/And the end of all our exploring/Will be to arrive where we started/And know the place for the first time."

What of Ignatius? Rather than becoming an Odyssey, his midlife journey took the shape of an Aeneid. His explorations finally took him to a new place and the unexpected task of founding a worldwide family of followers. In our day, one of them leads the Catholic Church as Pope Francis.

There are, of course, other ways to read the story of St. Ignatius Loyola after he was severely wounded on May 20, 1521. But reflecting on his midlife journey sheds much light on what happened.[2]

EXPERIENCES THAT SHAPED
THE SPIRITUAL EXERCISES

During the tedious weeks of convalescence at Loyola and a subsequent eleven-month stay at Manresa (near Barcelona), Ignatius went through various experiences that were to shape the Spiritual Exercises. By early 1523 and so at the end of eleven months of prayer in Manresa, he had already put down in writing the substance of the Exercises. Let me begin with one book that affected him.[3]

First, the minuscule library in the castle at Loyola included *The Golden Legend* by James of Voragine, a Dominican friar. Finished around 1265, *The Golden Legend* included many lives of Christian saints. Around one thousand manuscripts of the Latin text have survived and attest its enormous popularity. Reading this work led Ignatius to dreaming that he could imitate such saints as Dominic, Francis, and others—an experience that left him spiritually satisfied and consoled. Other daydreams, while pleasant at the time, did not yield such lasting satisfaction—specifically, dreams of performing wonderful deeds in the service of a noble lady, probably Catalina, the sister of the Emperor Charles V. Ignatius experienced a play of feelings: on the one hand, spiritually satisfying feelings that lasted, and, on the other hand, pleasant feelings that soon proved less than fully encouraging and life-giving.

The various kinds of daydreams that came to Ignatius prompted him into distinguishing between feelings of "consolation" and those of "desolation." He composed two sets of rules for "the discernment of spirits," which have their central place in the practice of the Spiritual Exercises and to which we come in the next chapter.

Second, it would be a mistake to ignore the chivalrous and noble ideals that helped fashion the daydreams Ignatius indulged about Princess Catalina. The courtesy of his time and culture properly colored important items that would be deployed in the Exercises: notably, the contemplation on the Kingdom of Christ (SpEx 91–99), including the offering made in the presence of the heavenly court (SpEx 98), and the meditation on Two Standards, the standard of "our commander-in-chief," Jesus Christ, and that of our deadly enemy, Lucifer (SpEx 136–48). Ignatius called for strict courtesy in using the Three Ways of Praying (SpEx 238–60) and, more generally, in the "additional" practices that support a reverent attention to God in prayer (SpEx 73–90). This spiritual courtesy of Ignatius remains desirable and effective for those who wish to move ahead in their life of prayer.

Third, Ludolph of Saxony's *Life of Christ* had a major influence on Ignatius's experience during his convalescence and how he shaped the text of the Exercises. From 1472, this work of a Carthusian monk was to enjoy sixty editions, but it has only recently for the first time been fully introduced and translated from the original Latin into English by Milton Walsh.[4] During the months at home in Loyola, Ignatius copied out selections from Ludolph's work, filling three hundred pages.

The meditations proposed by Ignatius for the Second, Third, and Fourth Weeks of the Spiritual Exercises, along with the "Mysteries of the Life of Christ Our Lord" (SpEx 261–312), follow the sequence laid down in Ludolph's *Life of Christ*. That includes the appearances of the risen Christ to his Mother (SpEx 299) and to Joseph of Arimathea (SpEx 310), neither of which are recorded in the New Testament and both of which have a chapter devoted to them in the *Life of Christ*.

Like other medieval writers, Ludolph encouraged his readers to imagine the events recorded in the Gospels and put themselves into the scene. They were not to hurry through Christ's life but to "take a small section each day." To draw closer to Jesus, they were to picture in their mind's eye something the Lord said or did and "simply talk with him." Thus they would become "become more familiar with him." Thinking "always somehow about Jesus," they could "strive to imitate him more closely and love him more deeply."[5] The advice about talking with Jesus, or what Ignatius called a "colloquy" (SpEx 53, for example), and about the imitation of Christ (SpEx 109) was incorporated into the Exercises.

Fourth, Ignatius followed the Christ-centeredness of Ludolph and utterly focused the Exercises on Jesus. The three questions Ignatius put in the First Week sum this up: "What have I done for Christ? What am I doing for Christ? What ought I to do for Christ?" (SpEx 53).

During his stay at Manresa, Ignatius discovered the *Imitation of Christ* by Thomas à Kempis. He also became familiar with, or at least more attached to, the *Anima Christi*, the Christ-focused prayer that begins "Soul of Christ" (SpEx 253, 258).

What Ignatius experienced and practiced at Loyola and Manresa backed up the advice he would give for the practice of the Exercises, as well as for life after the Exercises had been completed: "for the Second Week, as well as for the future, it is very helpful to read from time to time from the *Imitation of Christ*, or from the Gospels, or lives of saints [read: *The Golden Legend*]" (SpEx 100).

Inevitably Ignatius was drawn to make a pilgrimage to the Holy Land.[6] But he found that it was impossible to spend the rest of his life where Jesus was born, preached, died, and rose from the dead. After years of study and prayer, Ignatius arrived in Rome in late 1537. In a vision that came to him in a church at La Storta, a village just outside the eternal city, he saw himself being "placed with the Son" by the Father and assured that God would be "propitious" to him in Rome.

The Jesus-centeredness of Ignatius would find its public expression in his founding of the Society of Jesus, which enjoys as its titular feast the Most Holy Name of Jesus (January 4). In Ignatius's account of the mysteries of Christ's life, for January 1 he picked out the naming of Jesus: "his name was called Jesus, whereby he was called by the angel before he was conceived in the womb" (SpEx 266). After his death, Ignatius came to be buried in the church named after Jesus, the "Chiesa del Gesù" in downtown Rome. In that church you can see over 130 times on the walls and ceiling the classical abbreviation for the name of Jesus, the monogram IHS. Ignatius's Exercises and his legacy are all of one piece in calling on the exercitants to speak to Jesus and use his name. Jesus is Lord; Jesus is King; Jesus is our everything.

Fifth, that vision fostered the desire to remain in Rome and found the Society of Jesus. "Ordering" his life in accordance with the divine will was a question that had opened up during his convalescence in Loyola. The question found its counterpart in the Exercises and advice concerned with the "election" of one's vocation or, at least, with the reform of a life already chosen (SpEx 169–88).

Thus in at least five ways, Ignatius's foundational experiences at Loyola (mid-1521 to early 1523) fed into his great gift to the Christian Church, the fashioning and practice of the Spiritual Exercises.

We turn now to the text of the Exercises. We begin with explanations that Ignatius offered to those who came to "make retreats" and those who guided them as "directors."

2

EXPLANATIONS, PRACTICES, EXAMEN, AND DISCERNMENT

In the unsettled religious environment of the early sixteenth century, Ignatius wanted to clarify from the start what he was proposing for those who make the Spiritual Exercises. He introduced the work with twenty "annotations" or "notes" to explain what he expected from those who directed the Exercises and from those doing them. He did not think that he could improve the world by writing a book or delivering a wonderful speech, like Charlie Chaplin's call for freedom and mutual respect at the end of *The Great Dictator*. But Ignatius certainly believed that enormous improvements in Christian life (and human life generally) could come from those who let God deliver them from "unfreedoms"—Ignatius called them "disordered attachments" (SpEx 1)—and make the Exercises with total generosity.

This chapter respects the intentions of Ignatius by starting with his "annotations" or preliminary explanations. It will also examine what he said about "the additional practices" (SpEx 73–90), the "general examen" (SpEx 32–43) and "discernment of spirits" (SpEx 313–36). All these items not only shed light on the prayer and reflection he expected from exercitants but can also generate Christian living worthy of the name. They enjoy considerable value within the Exercises and beyond.

THE TWENTY ANNOTATIONS OR EXPLANATIONS (SpEx 1–20)

First, the opening annotation takes its bearings from a broad account of what spiritual exercises mean. They denote "every way" of examining one's conscience, "of meditating, contemplating, praying vocally and mentally, and other spiritual activities" (SpEx 1). Naming first *examining one's conscience* and putting it ahead of "meditating, contemplating, praying vocally and mentally" should seem startling. It is a conclusive reason for highlighting the importance for Ignatius of what he called "the examen," to which we come below.

Before ending the first, all-encompassing annotation, Ignatius should also startle readers by disclosing a specific aim as being primary for the Spiritual Exercises. He switches to a particular agenda, and announces that the Exercises prepare people to be liberated from all "disordered attachments." Then they will be able to seek and find what God wants from them—always for their lasting good. As Piccarda Donati says in the *Divine Comedy* of Dante, "in his [God's] will is our peace" (*Paradiso*, canto 3).[1]

Here we should stress "disordered" in "disordered attachments." Without healthy, loving attachments to our parents, siblings, and various others, there can be no human and Christian growth and life. We can adapt the famous dictum of Philip Larkin and say: what will survive of us are healthy attachments. Such attachments are not "disordered."

Ignatius seems to have taken it for granted that everyone's freedom was limited, since they suffered from disordered desires or what he calls "wrong attachments." Having broached the theme in the very first annotation, he returned to it in the sixteenth. He knew that only God can give "a right direction to one's desires," and set us free to desire and keep things for the sole motive that they are for "the service, honor, and glory of the Divine Majesty" (SpEx 16).

Ignatius does not ask that retreatants quietly suppress their feelings and attachments. But he wants them not to be secret slaves and, with the divine help, to be liberated from wrong attachments.

The Gospels supply examples of disordered attachments that block the invitation to follow Jesus. Abundant wealth stops the rich man, at least for the time being, from accepting the invitation to let following Jesus become his final destiny (Mark 10:17–22). Clinging to a past shaped by their wrong version of a theological legacy from Abraham and Sarah, some of Jesus' audience cannot hear the truth that "will set them free." They even turn toward killing Jesus (John 8:31–38).

A second highlight in Ignatius's spiritual pedagogy conveys the conviction that the director should simply summarize the material for meditation or contemplation and offer only brief explanations. The exercitant's personal reflection, supported by "the enlightenment of divine grace," will throw more light on the points for prayer. In a way that is "gratifying and spiritually profitable," this will bring home its meaning more than if the director had tried to explain at length the topic (SpEx 2).

This advice prompts Ignatius into offering a general observation about life that remains as accurate and relevant as ever: "it is not so much knowledge that fills and satisfies the soul [read: human spirit], but rather the intimate feeling and relishing of things" (SpEx 2). Those who treasure Dante Alighieri know that on September 14, 2021, we celebrated the 700th anniversary of his death. The opening lines of his *Divine Comedy* carry a wealth of meaning that fills and satisfies the human spirit: "In the middle of our life's journey I found myself in a dark wood, the straight way ahead lost." This world classic ends by celebrating the divine "love that moves the sun and the other stars." "Intimate feeling and relishing" describe common reactions to many of the utterly memorable passages of the *Divine Comedy*.

For those who ponder them prayerfully, the words of the inspired Scriptures can do that and more than that. The inspired word will fill and satisfy them, as "the eyes of their hearts become enlightened" (Eph 1:18, my translation).

Third, Ignatius quickly makes it clear that, faced with the complexities of human nature and its operation, his deepest concern is with the will rather than with the intellect—with what people want more than with what they know or reason about (SpEx 3). He encourages their desire to make the Exercises with total generosity; then "the Divine Majesty" can dispose of them and shape their lives (SpEx 5).

Fourth, Ignatius's courteous instincts emerge when he urges ever "greater reverence"—what we might call "reverential love"—when speaking face-to-face with God (SpEx 3), whom he repeatedly calls "the Divine Majesty" (for example, SpEx 106, 108). This sense of reverence will support the organized way in which the exercitants approach and give themselves to the hours of prayer. We return to this when we discuss "Practices."

The experience of Ignatius supported a fifth point, a firm trust that "the Creator and Lord will communicate himself" to people of faith who are searching for the divine will to guide their lives. God will "inflame" in them "love and praise," disposing them toward the ways in which they "will be better able to serve in the future." This means that directors should not self-indulgently show their own spiritual preferences. "Remaining in the middle like the point of a balance, they should leave the Creator to work directly with the creature, and the creature with the Creator and Lord" (SpEx 15). This conviction that God will "inflame" the exercitants with his "love and praise," communicating himself to and working directly with them, forms the most radical presupposition for those who give and those who make the Exercises.

Sixth, and remarkably, Ignatius detected no conflict with other preliminary remarks about directors taking the initiative to adapt the Exercises to the age, education, intelligence, and health of people (SpEx 18). But those decisions made by directors come, at least partly, before the Exercises begin. As such they do not substitute for God's interior "work" with the exercitants.

Likewise, Ignatius has instructions for those persons who cannot free themselves to make the Exercises full time but can set aside an hour and a half each day (SpEx 19). In the twentieth century, such "retreats in daily life" have flourished and brought remarkable spiritual results. A mature-age seminarian discovered the possibility of this way of doing the Exercises and asked me to direct him. Shaped by "annotation 19," his "retreat in daily life" lasted for a year and a half and solidified his decision to seek ordination to the priesthood. As an admirable parish priest, he has led several large communities in the Hispanic world.

After the COVID-19 pandemic struck and spread beginning in late 2019, many enterprising directors of the Spiritual Exercises have used Zoom to organize retreats in daily life. Some people who existed on the verge of spiritual defeat have found renewal through the unexpected chance of being enriched and strengthened by this mode of making the Spiritual Exercises. Let me give one example. A young priest, while engaged in his doctoral studies, organized six batches online for the Spiritual Exercises that were to last for two years. Nearly one thousand retreatants signed up, and nearly one hundred directors accompanied them.

Ignatius preferred exercitants, if they could, to disengage themselves completely from their normal life. He knew what then became possible: "the more we are alone and by ourselves, the more capable we become of drawing near to and reaching our Creator and Lord, and the more we reach him, the more we make ourselves ready to receive graces and gifts from the divine and supreme Goodness" (SpEx 20). Ignatius's year-long experience of life in a cave at Manresa confirmed this unqualified conviction about what the self-communicating God would do by way of "inflaming" people with love and "working directly" with them and within them (see SpEx 15).

The opening annotations include much about "consolation" and "desolation" and the need to discern in such spiritual movements the good or evil "spirits" that can inspire them (SpEx 6–10, 12–14, 17). We take up these themes at the end of this chapter.

This opening section of chapter 2 has selected for reflection eight of the annotations. More than any other part of the Exercises, the twenty annotations do justice to what this book expected from directors and exercitants. Here and in all that follows it is essential to read the full texts and not remain content with the comments I offer.

ADDITIONS OR ADDITIONAL PRACTICES

Ignatius, like everyone who practices a life of generous prayer, knew that it is only up to a certain point that we can control what happens at the time of prayer. Distractions may flood in; God can take over and lead us in directions we had not anticipated; we may doze off into sleep. But we always have a certain control over what precedes and what follows an hour of meditation or contemplation. We can always sign in and sign off prayer with attention to what we are about. This practice promises to bring us more completely what we "desire" (SpEx 73). (Here once again Ignatius's characteristic stress on our human will and its desires shows up.)

Those who reverence deeply the awesome presence of our Creator and Lord will resonate with the holy and serious etiquette with which Ignatius surrounds the time of prayer. The "additions" propose practices that may be demanding but that will stop exercitants from drifting away into a spiritual emptiness (SpEx 73–90).

Ignatius opens the list of practices by recommending that, after going to bed, we think of the time when we will rise and of what we will take to prayer (SpEx 73). That practice obviously opens the way for the theme(s) of the morning prayer to have some control over the play of mind and feelings that unconsciously takes place even while we sleep. The Nobel laureate Ernest Hemingway (d. 1961) has not been the only great writer to effectively adopt something similar. At times he put into his head some ideas aimed at creating and shaping what he was about to write. The mysterious processes at work even while he slept contributed to what he found himself writing in the morning.

Second, Ignatius asks retreatants to turn their attention, as soon as they wake and start dressing, to what they are going to meditate or contemplate. He suggests using imaginative comparisons drawn from a royal court or a legal court of his time (SpEx 74). We might also use a verse of some suitable hymn or a line from Sacred Scripture. Reflecting on some relevant work of art might also achieve the desired effect of concentrating our thoughts.

Third, Ignatius brings our body into his final recommendation when starting prayer: "one or two paces before the place where I have to meditate or contemplate, I shall stand for the space of an Our Father, with my mind raised up to consider how God our Lord looks at me, and then make a genuflection or other act of humility" (SpEx 75). Exercitants are to use their bodies as they insert themselves into a scene in which God "looks at me."

Fourth, along with the human will ("what I want"), our bodies are heavily involved in the next "additional practice." Kneeling, lying on my back, prostrate on the ground, seated, or standing (but not walking), I should always be "intent on the search for what I want" (SpEx 76). Here Ignatius stresses our search for God, which responds to God "working directly" with us (SpEx 15). "If I find what I want when kneeling," Ignatius adds, "I shall go no further, and similarly if prostrate etc....at the point at which I find what I want, I shall settle down, without any anxiety about going further until I have had my fill" (SpEx 76). This is a wise warning to take our time, be filled with God's grace, and avoid any desire to rush through all the material. Rushed prayer can only become increasingly thin.

Fifth, the possibility of walking occurs next, when Ignatius proposes fifteen minutes of reflection to come after prayer and be spent either seated or walking. If the contemplation or meditation has gone badly, the exercitants should look for the reasons and aim at doing better in the future. If the prayer has gone well, they should thank God and follow the same approach next time (SpEx 77). Ignatius puts a stark alternative: either the prayer has gone badly and has little to show for it. Or, with God's grace, it has gone well, and we should be grateful.

Sixth and finally, the additions conclude with recommendations about fasting and other penitential practices. Fasting, in particular, has survived in our modern world. The link between "prayer and fasting," made in traditional translations at the end of the story of a boy being delivered from an unclean spirit, continues to echo in the Christian memory (Mark 9:29). Scenes of people starving and dying in famines have encouraged the faithful to pray, fast, and use their savings to alleviate suffering in the world. Prayer in a global horizon, whether within the Spiritual Exercises or beyond, underscores links with a world still scourged by poverty and hunger.

THE GENERAL EXAMEN OF CONSCIENCE AND CONSCIOUSNESS

What Ignatius says about the "general examination of conscience" (SpEx 32–43) or "examination of consciousness" (as George Aschenbrenner has helpfully proposed) enjoys a long prehistory. "Know yourself" can sum up the best of Greek wisdom. As Socrates said, "an unexamined life is not worth living." In the letter that came closest to his writing an autobiography, St. Paul ended with this advice: "Examine yourselves to see whether you are living in the faith. Test yourselves" (2 Cor 13:5). Prayerfully examining and testing one's daily experience remains critically important, not only during the Spiritual Exercises but also in ordinary life. Ignatius's method for doing so remains one the lasting gems of the Exercises. It covers five points (SpEx 43).

First, the exercitants should give thanks to God for all the benefits they have received. We meet such gratitude resoundingly expressed in psalms of praise (as in Pss 145—50), in the *Benedictus*, *Magnificat*, and *Nunc Dimittis* with which Luke opens his Gospel, and at the end of the Exercises. The Contemplation for Attaining Love knows how God shares with me (SpEx 234) and "labors for me" in all creatures upon the face of the earth (SpEx 236).

Second, Ignatius wants the exercitants to ask for the grace "to know my sins" and to rid myself of them. "Knowing," far from being an end in itself, carries something of the biblical sense of experiencing—here in the sense of providing the means for moving to real freedom, through knowing at depth and in one's feelings. Far from keeping sin and evil at an intellectual distance, such knowing involves "receiving an interior knowledge of my sins and an *abhorrence* of them," feeling "a sense of the *disorder* in my actions, so that *abhorring* it I may amend my life and put order into it" (SpEx 63).

The language of "interior knowledge" will recur positively in the prayer for "the interior knowledge of the Lord who became human for me" (SpEx104). This prayer will be filled out when asking for "what I want" in the Contemplation for Attaining Love (SpEx 233).

Ignatius does not appeal here to Paul's letters, but the knowledge he has in mind finds support in the apostle's prayer: "that your love overflow more and more in knowledge and full insight, so that you may discern the things that really matter" (Phil 1:9–10, my translation). In his Letter to the Romans, Paul had already exhorted the faithful: "be transformed by the renewal of your minds, so that you may discern what is the will of God—what is good and acceptable and perfect" (12:2). Such knowledge is a wisdom "not of this world" but comes from God (see 1 Cor 2:7, 20).

The knowing that Ignatius has in mind takes a double and very practical form in the meditation on the Two Standards. On the one hand, the exercitants should "ask for knowledge of the deceptions practiced by the evil leader [Lucifer] and for help to guard against them." On the other hand, they should also ask "for knowledge of the true life revealed by the supreme and true Commander [Christ] and for grace to imitate him" (SpEx 139).

Significantly Ignatius will propose a "knowledge of *the world*, so that out of abhorrence for it, I may put away from myself *worldly* and aimless things" (SpEx 63; italics mine). Here "world" matches a Johannine characterization: "everything that is in the world is the desire of the flesh, the desire of the eyes, and the pride of life," "life" being understood not in the rich sense of everlasting life (*zōē*) but in the sense of mere biological life (*bios*) (1 John 2:16). To be sure, Jesus came to save "the whole world" (1 John 2:2). But this is also the world of a false love for wealth and honors, of passions that separate people from God and from one another, and of "*alazonia*" or arrogance, boasting and self-justification.[2]

The context of the Exercises should prompt us into a fuller reading of what Ignatius intends by a "knowledge of sins" when explaining the general examen. His language is cryptic but can be filled out by what later sections add.

Third, a "review" that follows is easily the longest item in Ignatius's list of five points for the examen. It does not mention as such any experiences of temptation, sin, and infidelity, but it asks for careful reflection on what I have thought, said, and done up to the time of the examen. We can profitably translate this invitation in terms of divine "epiphanies" and human "responses." How has God been revealed in the thoughts, feelings, words, and deeds that have made up all that I have experienced? To what extent have my thoughts, words, and deeds responded to these divine "epiphanies"? Have service and love characterized my response?

When Ignatius reflects on our thoughts, words, and deeds, some of what he says proves time-conditioned (SpEx 32–42). But some of his remarks remain as pertinent as ever: for example, his warnings against "defamation" and "spreading gossip" (SpEx 41) and his appeal to the Ten Commandments as standards of behavior (SpEx 42).

Fourth, recovering in this way the immediate past, we should ask "pardon" for what has been sinful. Gratitude for the divine "epiphanies" in my daily life would, very appropriately, accompany this request for forgiveness. Thanksgiving for what God has done and continues to do for me powerfully motivates "identifying" ourselves as repentant sinners.

Fifth and finally, a resolution to do better naturally concludes the examen. We can hope that we will enjoy a new sense of God's creative presence in our lives, which prompts a new commitment to act in loving freedom toward our Creator and Lord.

We should not miss the way Ignatius recommends ending with an Our Father, the first time the Exercises mention the prayer given to us by Jesus. As we shall see, it will play a frequent part in what follows and was deeply treasured by Ignatius himself.

DISCERNMENT OF GOOD AND EVIL SPIRITS

The earliest Christians knew the spiritual battle that they faced: "Our struggle is not against enemies of flesh and blood, but against the rulers, against the authorities, against the cosmic powers of the present darkness, against the spiritual forces of evil in the heavenly places" (Eph 6:12). Set against such evil spirits, the good angels of God continued to play their role (Matt 1:20–24; 28:2–7, for example).

Ignatius had no difficulty about identifying the "good and evil spirits" as, respectively, good angels and fallen angels, led by Lucifer. Today many Christians prefer to speak of life-giving and deceptive forces. But as Juliet asked in Shakespeare's *Romeo and Juliet* (act 2, scene 2), "what's in a name?" It is the mysterious impulses that should hold our attention more than any names we give them.

After touching early in the Exercises on the question of the discernment of spirits (SpEx 4, 6–10, 17), Ignatius set out fourteen rules that could be more suitable for such discerning in the first week (SpEx 313–27) and eight rules that would be suitable for the second week (328–36). We sample here some of the rules for the first week, leaving Ignatius's further rules and remarks to be read by those who give and those who make the Exercises.

First, the good and evil spirits make themselves known in movements of "consolation" and "desolation." Ignatius describes consolation as expressing itself in impulses to love our Creator and Lord, in tears that lead to that love, and a sense of interior happiness which brings quiet and peace (SpEx 316). Desolation involves darkness, anxiety arising from temptations, a lack of confidence, and a sense of sadness, as though we were "cut off from God" (SpEx 317). Some of the psalms of lamentation, such as Psalm 22, the opening words of which Jesus quoted on the cross, bring to life vividly such desolation. But we are never in fact cut off from God, who is always "closer to us than we are to ourselves" (*"interior intimo meo,"* St. Augustine, *Confessions,* 3.6.11). It is with poetically challenging detail that Psalm 139 unpacks this uniquely intimate nearness of God.

Second, in such time of desolation, so Ignatius insists, we should never make any change in the resolutions or decisions we have already made. In that state it is the evil spirit who seeks to "guide and counsel us." Just as the good spirit guides us more in consolation, so in desolation it is the evil spirit who works at advising and guiding us. "By following the counsels" of the evil spirit, Ignatius warns, "we can never find the right way" (SpEx 318).

Third, Ignatius does, however, recommend one form of change: counterattack. In the annotations he had already drawn attention to the way in which "the enemy usually leaves nothing undone in his efforts" to prompt us into shortening the hour to be spent on each of the five periods of meditation or contemplation. Ignatius recommends that the exercitants react by spending a little more than the full hour at prayer. In this way they will not only stand up to "the adversary" but even "overthrow" him (SpEx 12–13). Faced with desolation, they should "make an intense effort" to oppose it, by insisting more on prayer and other spiritual means (SpEx 319).

Fourth, Ignatius is serenely confident that God's help remains with those suffering from desolation, "even though they may not clearly feel it." "Although the Lord has withdrawn their great fervor, deeply felt love, and intense grace," he has still left them sufficient grace to cope with this period of trial (SpEx 320).

Moses met God not only at the burning bush (Exod 3:1–6) but also in "the thick darkness" on Mount Sinai (Exod 20:21). The meaning of light/fire and darkness has always proved rich and complex. But, among other things, the symbolism of Moses's story encourages us to engage intensely with God in darkness, as well as in light. The experience of God "in the thick darkness" was no less fruitful for Moses than meeting God by the light of a burning bush. We may grow more spiritually in the darkness of desolation than in the light of consolation.

Fifth, Ignatius calls on those doing the Exercises to be *patient* in time of desolation. Consolation will come again (SpEx 321). Here he aligned himself with a characteristic piece of advice we find widely distributed in the New Testament: "to be patient (*hyomenein*)." Years ago a spiritual director in Germany called it "being able to tough it out" and delighted me with the word he used: "*das Durchhaltenkönnen.*"

Sixth, Ignatius proposes three reasons why exercitants might find themselves "desolated." That state may be due to their faults; it may be God testing them; or it may be to help them understand "that everything is a gracious gift from God" (SpEx 322). The spirituality of Eastern Christianity expresses the second reason vividly: God "breaks all our bones" when putting us together again and remaking us. We die to our pasts so that new life can break through. As regards the third reason, no one has summed it up more powerfully than Georges Bernanos at the end of *The Diary of a Country Priest.* A young curate, dying of cancer after a seemingly useless ministry in a spiritually cancerous village, murmurs to his nonbelieving friend: "all is grace."

Seventh, retreatants, when feeling deeply consoled, should remember that consolation is not our achievement but a gift from God. In any case, desolation will arrive at some point (SpEx 323–24). Here Ignatius is speaking like a grateful realist and not like a pessimist.

I have selected seven pieces of advice that Ignatius offers toward dealing with experiences of desolation and consolation. He is bent on leading exercitants to detect where evil spirits may be working to corrupt and destroy them and where God is leading them on their spiritual pilgrimage.

All the items presented in this chapter apply both to the experience of the Spiritual Exercises and to the struggles of daily Christian living. We take up now the four weeks of the Exercises and what Ignatius proposes for the prayerful attention of the exercitants.

FIRST WEEK

3

PRINCIPLE AND FOUNDATION

The "Principle and Foundation" (SpEx 23; hereafter PF) comes right at the start of the First Week and is presented without any preparatory prayer or concluding "colloquy."[1] Unlike other parts of the Exercises, there is no clear instruction about using the PF. We know that the text was added late to the Spiritual Exercises.[2] It has links to earlier material (such as Annotations 1, 15, and 16), and was obviously meant to dispose people toward making the Spiritual Exercises. It did this by questioning them on the God whom Ignatius characteristically called "Our Lord" and "Creator," our Lord through being our Creator.

By the late 1530s, Ignatius's experience of directing the Exercises had shown him the need to check the image of God that prospective retreatants brought with them. For instance, it was crucial that they could focus and ruminate on God's whole plan for created realities and especially for human beings. This would enable them to deliberate on the state of life to which God called them (SpEx 135, 169–89). Radical God-centeredness, even passionate attachment to God, remains essential for any well-founded decision-making.

More broadly, the PF provides a big picture of what faith and human existence is about—the absolute priority of God. From the point of view of the Spiritual Exercises themselves, we find elements of the PF present not only in the rules for election (SpEx 169–89) but also in preparatory prayers (SpEx 46, for example), the triple colloquy of the First Week (SpEx 62), the Two Standards

(SpEx 136–48), the Three Classes of Persons (SpEx 149–57), Three Kinds of Humility (SpEx 165-8), and the Contemplation for Attaining Love (SpEx 230-37). The PF draws together much that will show up in the Spiritual Exercises. One might even interpret the PF as a vision statement that covers their core values.

Some modern writers put dramatically the question that lay behind the PF: God, who are you for me? Thus the 1997 book by Gerard W. Hughes was entitled *God, Where Are You?* His earlier work, which won the Collins book award, was called *The God of Surprises* (1991). More recently Richard Leonard published *Where the Hell Is God?* (2010).[3]

Exercitants need to be sure of God before entering the First Week proper and facing the hard truths, for example, about sin. Who is the God coming into immediate contact with me, a sinner (Annotation 15)? God exists "for me" and wishes to share as much as possible with me. The will of God and my best interests coincide.

PF summarizes the dispositions necessary to commence the First Week. Without these basics being firmly grounded in the exercitants, no progress is possible. It is not a matter of mere intellectual reasoning but an attitude of mind *and heart*, something to be intimately felt and relished (SpEx 2).

This chapter will reproduce the PF to facilitate reflection on the text. I will then offer four further, extended comments before suggesting a certain connection between the PF and the marriage vows accepted in early sixteenth-century Europe. In the PF, at least implicitly, "love was in the air."

THE TEXT AND FOUR COMMENTS

The text of the PF runs as follows:

The human person is *created* to praise, reverence and serve God Our Lord, and by so doing to save his or her soul. The other things on the face of the earth are *created* for human beings in order to help them pursue the end for which they are *created*. It follows from this that one must use other *created* things insofar as they help toward one's end and free oneself from them insofar as they are obstacles to one's end. To do this we need to make ourselves indifferent to all *created* things, provided the matter is subject to our own free choice and there is no prohibition. Thus as far as we are concerned, we should not want health more than illness, wealth more than poverty, fame more than disgrace, a long life rather than a short one, and similarly for all the rest. But we should desire and choose only what helps us more toward the end for which we are *created*. (SpEx 23; italics mine)

First, introducing italics helps us spot Ignatius's primary stress on God as Creator. While the PF never names God as "Creator," it refers three times to human beings as "created" and three times to "other created things." This establishes a kind of "creation spirituality" for all human beings and makes the PF a key text for possible interreligious dialogue.[4] It offers a common way toward spiritual freedom, based on a true relationship between creatures and the Creator. What both Ignatius and Gandhi propose share in the common light of creation.

Second, Oxford University Press has continued to publish a highly successful series of short books: *Very Short Introductions*. They cover areas of human study (for example, in philosophy and history), figures in history (including Jesus), and all manner of interesting and even centrally important questions, including "the meaning of life." What Gandhi twice calls our "ultimate aim," Ignatius four times names as "the end [purpose] for which we are created." This ultimate meaning of our life takes a double form: on the one hand, "to praise, reverence and serve God our Lord," and, on the other hand, "by so doing to save our souls."

"Saving our souls" is a classic but now antiquated way of describing the final salvation of human beings as a whole, in *both* their bodily and spiritual components. Just occasionally this "holistic" sense of saving souls lingers on when the journalists or historians report a shipwreck or an emergency plane landing on water and declare that so many "souls," that is to say "people," were, nevertheless, saved.

What surprises people can be the absence of "love" in the triad "praise, reverence and serve God." Earlier in the Exercises, as we saw in the previous chapter, Ignatius had already spoken of God inflaming "love and praise" in retreatants (SpEx 15). Why does he not repeat this language in the PF? He will take up the language of love in the reflection on a wonderful, human king to whom we should "respond in a spirit of love" (SpEx 97). My last chapter suggested reading "reverence" (SpEx 3) as "reverential love." Eventually such "loving reverence" will bring retreatants to the Contemplation for Attaining Love and the prayer to be enabled to "love and serve" the Divine Majesty in all things (SpEx 230–37). The "reverence" of which the PF speaks is not alien to love.

The reverential love toward God proposed by Ignatius coincides at least partly with what Rudolf Otto indicated about the "holy" God as the *"mysterium tremendum et fascinans* (the awesome and fascinating mystery)."[5] Abraham and Sarah were drawn toward the mystery of the Lord present to them in the form of three angelic visitors, but also awestruck by the same mystery (Gen 18:1–15). The experience of Moses in his call from God (Exod 2:23—4:17) blended reverential fear with a loving desire to be with God and do what the Lord wanted. Peter's reaction to the great catch of fish (Luke 5:1–11) symbolized how penitent astonishment joined with loving delight over what the generous Savior had done for him.

A similar solution may be offered when Ignatius states that "one must *use* other created things insofar as they help toward one's end and free oneself from them insofar as they are obstacles to one's end" (italics mine). This language of "using" can easily suggest a cold, calculating, even manipulative relationship to the human beings and other creatures that provide the setting for our life. What room is left for the human responses of interest, love, enjoyment, deep compassion, and other spontaneous feelings?

Ignatius himself obviously felt no such tension, as we can gather from interpreting the language of the PF within the context of the entire Exercises. The colloquy with Christ hanging on the cross invites the exercitants to react with deep, personal feeling (SpEx 53). As the Second Week begins and we come to the contemplation on the incarnation, Ignatius wants the retreatants to "ask for interior knowledge of the Lord who became human for me so that I may better *love* and follow him" (SpEx 104; italics mine). In the Fourth Week, the Contemplation for Attaining Love opens by evoking the world of "the lover" and "the beloved" (SpEx 230).

Third, the last chapter noted the primacy that Ignatius assigned to the will over the intellect (SpEx 3). The heading that introduces the First Week emphasizes free will by speaking of "overcoming," "ordering," "decision," and "freedom" (SpEx 21). The PF repeatedly reflects this primacy: human beings are to "pursue the aim for which they are created," they are "to free themselves" from what hinders that aim by making themselves "indifferent to all created things," and they "should not want health more than illness, wealth rather than poverty," and so forth. In short, they "should desire and choose only what helps more toward" their end.

In the PF's picture of human beings searching for God and what they should do on that search, is God's search for us honored and the priority of the divine grace over our efforts? Yes, the priority of God's search and grace endures; we are called to be constantly open, in Ignatius's sense of active "indifference," to all the ways in which God wishes to share with us. To be truly free we must give up the desire to control our life and must place ourselves unreservedly in the hands of God.

The contemplations and meditations of the Exercises, by constantly asking for divine grace, witness to the primacy of God's search for us. The PF fits into the whole picture by paying tribute to our subordinate and responsive search for God. The Gospel of John does something similar. On the one hand, using a fishing term for dragging in a net, Jesus declares, "No one can come to me unless the Father haul him" (John 6:44, my translation). But, on the other hand, Jesus respects the human search and questions his first disciples: "What are you looking for?" (John 1:38). The PF spells out what we should be looking for.

Fourth, we might sum up two central contributions of the PF. (1) Making the Spiritual Exercises is a way to freedom, real freedom based on truth. The PF sets out the basic truth of existence in terms of human commitment and activity. Other passages of the Exercises reflect on the divine commitment to us and activity for us. (2) In the immediate context of the First Week, the PF can prevent unhealthy introspection or self-centered shame. The grace of the First Week involves responding with thanks to the God who loves me so much.

Let me complete my comments on the PF by sharing something from its historical context that encourages interpreting it in terms of love.

MARRIAGE VOWS IN THE PRINCIPLE AND FOUNDATION

In his lectures on the Spiritual Exercises, Anthony de Mello spoke lyrically of the Principle and Foundation (SpEx 23) but recognized how for some people—he mentioned Louis Evely—the "whole idea" of the PF is "ridiculous, unchristian, and pagan."[6] De Mello himself understood the thrust of the PF to be "falling in love with the Absolute."[7] Can we strengthen de Mello's argument by going beyond him and recognizing how marriage vows were echoed in the language of PF? Was the PF about falling in love and committing oneself in love to the Absolute? Did Ignatius, consciously or unconsciously, echo the language of marriage vows in the PF?

The outstanding commentary on the Spiritual Exercises by Santiago Arzubialde points out that the text of the PF evolved gradually, and notes echoes in the final version from works of Erasmus of Rotterdam and Peter Lombard.[8] But Arzubialde does not mention the possibility of contemporary marriage vows being echoed by Ignatius. Can we detect such echoes?

Late Medieval Marriage Vows

In their *Documents of the Marriage Liturgy*, Mark Searle and Kenneth W. Stevenson cite *The Sarum Manual*, the fifteenth-century rite from the church of Salisbury, which "was widely used in England and was influential beyond the British Isles." Exemplifying "the way marriage rites looked on the eve of the Reformation," the manual "reveals how the Anglo-Norman structures for public betrothal and public exchange of marriage consent had now been elaborated into a rich vernacular ceremony of consent." This liturgical service took place at the door of a church[9] and in the presence of priest and people.[10] The bridegroom took the hand of the bride as he pledged his "troth": "I, N., take thee, N., to be my weddyd wyfe, to haue and to holde [from this day forward], for better for wurs, for richer for porer, in syckenes and in helthe tyll deth us departe."[11] The bride then used similar language in pledging her "troth." This language envisaged four outcomes: a general outcome "for better for worse," which could involve particular outcomes: riches or poverty, sickness or health, and being united in life or separated by death.

Searle and Stevenson also reproduce selections from a fourteenth-century marriage rite from the Abbey of Barbeau, a Cistercian foundation in the diocese of Sens (central France). The bridegroom declared before the priest and people, "I take you to be my wife and my spouse and I pledge to you the faith of my body, that I will be faithful to you and loyal with my body and my goods, and that I will keep you *in sickness and in health* and in whatever condition it will please the Lord to place you, and that I will not exchange you *for better or worse until the end*."[12]

This language used in this ritual from the Abbey of Barbeau matches, albeit in a different order, three of the binary pairs found a century later in the *Sarum Manual*: sickness/health, better/worse, the end of life/death. One might also detect a discreet reference to riches/poverty being made in the language of "my goods." This earlier language for marriage consent in the Barbeau rite, while less complete than that found in the *Sarum Manual*, anticipates similar binary forms of commitment.

In *The Medieval Idea of Marriage*, Christopher Brooke drew on a fundamental study of marriage rituals found in twelfth-century "pontificals or missals deriving from Brittany, Normandy, and England." They prescribed that the groom receive the bride "in God's faith and his own, to be kept in health and sickness as long as she lives."[13] Their married relationship and life could bring health or sickness and the possibility of marriage ending with her death. The explicit outcomes envisaged by such twelfth-century rituals were only two, simpler than the scheme in *The Sarum Manual*.

Brooke reports the story of the marriage promises (between John Beke and a certain Marjory) being exchanged away from the church and without the benefit of clergy or any public ceremony. Taking her right hand, Beke said, "Marjory, here I take you as my wife, for better or worse, to have and to hold until the end of my life, and of this I give you my faith." Marjory then replied in the same words.[14] The simple language likewise envisaged only two outcomes: "better or worse," and life or "the end" of life through death. Here "better or worse" replaced "sickness and health."

The late medieval examples cited by Brooke are similar to but shorter than the fourfold possibilities spelled out in the *Sarum Manual*. This manual envisaged "for better for worse," "for richer for poorer," "in sickness and in health," "till death us do part [from a living relationship]."

Ignatius and the Language of Marriage Vows

In the PF, Ignatius teaches that "we should not want health more than sickness, wealth more than poverty, fame more than disgrace, a long life more than a short one" (SpEx 23).[15] Three of the four possibilities match the language of the *Sarum Manual*: "health/sickness" is matched by "in sickness and in health," "wealth/poverty" by "for richer for poorer," "long life/short life" by "till death us do part." Only Ignatius's characteristic "fame/disgrace" finds no counterpart in the language prescribed by the manual for the marriage ceremony.

I have not yet located studies of the language of marriage vows in the Spanish/Basque environment in which Ignatius grew up. But up to the time when he left Spain for France, he must have attended weddings of relatives, friends, or others, and heard the exchange of marriage vows. One would expect the language of those vows to have resembled that used in France and England. In fact, the study of marriage rituals by Mutembe and

Molin repeatedly shows how in various aspects marriage texts and customs from Toledo and elsewhere in Spain paralleled or at least resembled the French marriage rituals.

His move in 1528 to Paris put Ignatius in the context of marriage rituals presented by Brooke, Mutembe and Molin, and Searle and Stevenson. He was to study at the University of Paris until 1535, with begging journeys to England and Flanders in search of funds. It seems improbable that during those seven years Ignatius never witnessed any marriage ceremonies, which frequently took place at the door or in the porch of churches. This very public setting meant that even those who were simply passing by could see what was happening and hear what was being said at weddings. The existing pontificals, missals, and the internationally influential *Sarum Manual* match substantially, albeit not completely, the four binary outcomes envisaged by Ignatius.

The parallelism is striking and suggests that Ignatius's language in one section of the PF drew, consciously or unconsciously, from the traditional liturgical forms for expressing marriage consent to which he was exposed—probably during his life in Spain and certainly during seven years of life and study in Paris—before the PF took its final form around 1539 or a little later.

Here we need to refrain from lapsing into the intentional fallacy, which insists that texts mean only what their authors consciously intended to communicate. As the classical exponent of this theory, Eric Donald Hirsch put it, "a text means what its author meant."[16] Of course, we should establish and honor, to the extent that we can, the intention of the author—in this case, Ignatius, the author of the PF. Nevertheless, we should also look beyond the original authors for further meaning in the texts they produced.

Paul Ricoeur wrote, "The meaning of what has been written down is henceforth separate from the possible intentions of the authors[...]What we call the semantic autonomy of the text means that the text unfolds a history distinct from that of the author."[17] In short, "what the text signifies no longer coincides [simply] with what the author[s] meant."[18] Ricoeur cited the view of Hirsch and firmly rejected it: "The problem of the right understanding [of a text] can no longer be solved by a simple return to the alleged intention of an author."[19] Even when we can establish to our satisfaction what authors (Ignatius, for example) intended, their explicit intentions do not enjoy a one-sided privilege, let alone an exclusive role, when we interpret the texts they composed.

Hans-Georg Gadamer agrees: "Not just occasionally but always, the meaning of a text goes beyond its author." In repeating this point, he adds that texts also become independent from their original addressees: "The horizon of understanding cannot be limited either by what the writer originally had in mind, or by the horizon of the person to whom the text was originally addressed." Hence Gadamer could argue, "Reconstructing what the author really had in mind is at best a limited undertaking."[20]

In short, texts can communicate more than their authors consciously knew or meant. Hence I propose reading part of the text of the PF within the horizon of the language of marriage vows that Ignatius's world had inherited from late medieval usage.

The Theme of Love Already Present in the PF

Arzubialde, while aware that the PF does not explicitly use the language of love, names the "horizon" that Ignatius sketches as "implicitly that of a relation of the love of friendship between God and man." He cites what comes later in the second preamble to the Contemplation for Attaining Love, when the exercitant prays to "love and serve the Divine Majesty in everything" (SpEx 233). The "indifference" highlighted in the PF "is the result of the spiritual experience of God-Love," an indifference "full of affection."[21]

Arzubialde continues to expound the PF in the horizon of love. A remarkable footnote declares, "The experience of feeling oneself loved is the only [experience] that generates liberty."[22] "True liberty" comes through feeling oneself loved by God who is "Father and absolute security." The revelation of divine love allows us "to experience" the freedom to "incorporate positively [our] affections" in the service of God and the discovery of his will in all things." Using language that parallels what we quoted above from de Mello, Arzubialde speaks of "the Absolute" being manifested as "provident love and security."[23] Correspondingly, "indifference" means "loving obedience to the will of the Father."[24]

In support of his case for love and the horizon of love shaping the PF, Arzubialde repeatedly refers ahead to the Contemplation for Attaining Love—he points, for example, to Ignatius's theme of the "provident love of God" who "desires to give himself completely to human beings" (SpEx 234). In the light of the Contemplation, Arzubialde expounds this love as mutual "communication"—from God to human beings and from human beings to God.[25] He ends his commentary on the PF by presenting the PF and the Contemplation for Attaining Love as "complementary" visions of God's creative and salvific design.[26]

Arzubialde knows that the text of the PF does not explicitly mention love, not even mentioning that it will be treated later in the Spiritual Exercises. Yet he rightly introduces the horizon of love to explain the central thrust of the PF, an experience of being loved that creates the freedom to be totally God-centered and disposed to serve God in all things. He goes beyond any explicitly stated connections made by Ignatius and reads the PF in the light of what is placed at the end of Exercises, the Contemplation for Attaining love.

Even though the author (Ignatius) does not expressly draw the connection, Arzubialde reads one text written by Ignatius within the horizon of another text by the same author, and uncovers richer, latent meanings. This encourages me to read the section of the PF (about health/sickness, wealth/poverty, fame/disgrace, and long life/short life) in the light of texts not written by Ignatius but abundantly present in his world (the language of late medieval marriage vows). Doing this could reinforce the already persuasive case made by Arzubialde for reading the PF in the light of divine and human love, that mutual communication in which the lover and beloved give themselves to each other.

4

EXERCISES OF THE FIRST WEEK

Through the five exercises of the First Week of the Spiritual Exercises, St. Ignatius clarifies the way he expects the retreatants to prayerfully approach any such meditations, whether in the First Week or in the subsequent Second, Third, or Fourth Weeks. Here, in what he calls a meditation on the first, second, and third sins (SpEx 45–54), he sketches three steps that are involved.

THE FIRST EXERCISE

Three Steps

A preparatory prayer comes first, asking, "God our Lord for grace that all my intentions, actions and operations may be directed purely to the service and praise of his Divine Majesty" (SpEx 46). Although he does not say so here, Ignatius subsequently proposes that the same preparatory prayer be said before all the meditations (and contemplations) that follow in the Exercises (SpEx 55, 62, 65, 91, and so forth).

Second, Ignatius is well aware of the power of our imagination and how prayer can take shape around what he calls "the composition of place." What we imagine need not have the last word, but it certainly can condition our spiritual vision. Hence he asks the exercitants to entertain some picture or image that appropriately fits the meditation or contemplation they are starting. For meditating on sin, he wants those making the Exercises to see with their imagination "my soul imprisoned in this body, which will one day disintegrate, and my whole composite self [soul and body] as if exiled in this valley among the beasts" (SpEx 47).

This way of imagining my present existence introduces imprisonment, death and disintegration, exile, and the company of wild beasts. Ignatius echoes biblical and devotional images that can be thoroughly familiar. Mark's Gospel pictures Jesus during his forty-day "retreat" in the wilderness as being "with the wild beasts" (Mark 1:12–13). The *Salve Regina* prays to the Blessed Virgin Mary out of "this valley of tears."

The themes of death, exile, and imprisonment turn up repeatedly in the Psalms and in other inspired Scriptures, and in the Christian tradition. Jesus himself, albeit not using the term *exile*, pictured the self-imposed exile of the prodigal son suffering from hunger and living with unclean animals (Luke 15:15–17). Dante wrote memorably of the bitter experience of exile: "All stairs are steep when they belong/to other men, to climb or to descend" (*Paradiso*, canto 17).[1] In the twenty-first century over sixty million refugees and asylum seekers cast a suffering shadow over the history of the modern world and provide us with images of exile at its very worst—an imprisonment with no fixed term of sentence.

A holistic view of the human condition may dismiss the image of the soul imprisoned in the body as an unacceptable return to what Socrates and Plato championed. But that does not demolish the whole composition of place. We can select (and perhaps combine) other effective themes in what Ignatius offers for this first exercise. We can picture scenes of imprisonment, exile, and death—not to mention the valleys and mountains of our earth ravaged by climate change and its results. We need not keep Ignatius's entire composition of place at a distance. It contains numerous images of undiminished power.

Third, the last step before applying the intellect to meditation consists in asking "God for what I want and desire." Here that will mean "personal shame and confusion" on account of my numerous sins (SpEx 48). Ignatius does not look for mere conceptual clarity about sin, but for an affective knowledge, or what he calls "interior knowledge," of my sins (SpEx 63). That should be accompanied by intense feelings: "mounting and intense sorrow and [even] *tears* for my sins" (SpEx 55) and "an abhorrence for my sins" (SpEx 63).

Ignatius mentions "tears" as a proper reaction for those who feel "grief" over the sufferings of Christ in his passion (SpEx 48). Here it is rather a matter of tearful grief that sinners should feel when face-to-face with the crucified Christ. This should lead them to the colloquy with the crucified Jesus (SpEx 53; see below). The mysteries of Christ's life that Ignatius would eventually list for meditation or contemplation include Peter denying Christ and then weeping bitterly over this awful sin of cowardice (SpEx 292; Luke 22:62).

Three Points

For the composition of place and the prayer "for what I want and desire," Ignatius uses the term *preamble*, but not with a view to downplay them. Personally, I have always valued his high regard for preambles, since my maternal grandfather, Patrick McMahon Glynn, as an elected delegate to the Australian Federal Convention of 1897, successfully proposed as a preamble to the Australian Constitution the words "Humbly relying on the blessing of almighty God,..." Applying *preamble* to the opening words of the first-time constitution for a country differs, of course, from the use of *preamble* in the Spiritual Exercises. But a sense of radical significance underlies both usages.

Ignatius applies the term *points* to the matter for the opening meditation and to the matter for subsequent meditations and contemplations in the Exercises. He makes supremely clear what he recommends that retreatants take up in prayer; they will face few chances of losing their way.

The opening exercise of the First Week begins by applying our "three powers" of memory, intellect, and will—but not forgetting the imagination—to "the first sin," namely, the sin of the angels. Difficulties arise about the use of this material for meditation.

When the seventy-two disciples return from their mission, even though the instructions they had received from Jesus (Luke 10:1–12) made no mention of exorcising demons, they report with joy that in his name they had power over them. Referring either to this success on their mission or (perhaps) to an original fall from grace, he replies, "I saw Satan fall like lightning from heaven" (Luke 10:18). For the most part, teaching about some angels who, although created in grace, committed a sin that fixed them irrevocably in paradise or in eternal damnation came not from biblical revelation but from medieval theologians such as Thomas Aquinas. Some theologians (such as Duns Scotus) argued that angels had to commit a succession of evil acts before suffering such damnation.[2]

Ignatius wants retreatants to go over the fall of angels with understanding "and then stir up the heart's affections with the will" (SpEx 50). But a remote theme developed by medieval theologians in the aftermath of apocryphal Jewish speculations can hardly promise to move contemporary Christians to call to mind their "many sins" and feel deep "shame and confusion" over their sins (SpEx 50).

The second point of this exercise on sin turns to the sin of Adam and Eve, which, as the literary historian Stephen Greenblatt has gloriously illustrated, remains vigorously alive, if controversial, in the imagination of the Western world and beyond.[3] That sin, Ignatius insists, caused our first parents "long penance" and brought corruption "upon the human race, with so many people going their way toward hell" (SpEx 51).

In his third point Ignatius imagines a particular human being who finishes up in hell perhaps for a single mortal sin but also "numberless other people who have gone to hell for fewer sins than I have committed." Ignatius stresses the justice of this sentence to eternal damnation, given "the gravity and malice of sin" that acts against the "infinite goodness" of our Creator and Lord (SpEx 52) and says "no" to the meaning of creation. Ignatius is second to none in recognizing the catastrophe we meet in sin;

it destroys one's proper relationship with God, with oneself, with one another, and with the world.

At the end of this chapter we will offer some alternatives to the material Ignatius proposes for meditation on our sins and the mercy of God. But the "colloquy" or heart-to-heart conversation with Christ on the cross remains a nonnegotiable part of this meditation. Ignatius wants the retreatants to imagine "Christ Our Lord before me on the cross" and ask "how it came about that the Creator made himself man, and from eternal life came to temporal death, and thus to die for my sins." Then they should question themselves: "What have I done for Christ? What am I doing for Christ? What ought I do for Christ?" (SpEx 53–54).

Ignatius is far from being the only classical author to fashion three such radical questions—about the past, present, and future, respectively. At the end of his *Critique of Pure Reason*, Immanuel Kant, arguably the greatest German philosopher of all time, raised three questions that can open the way to carefully following a moral compass and contributing to the common good: "All interest of my reason (the speculative as well as the practical) is united in the following three questions: What can I know? What should I do? What may I hope for?"[4] Ignatius agrees with Kant in putting very personal questions: about what I can know, what I should do, and what I may hope for. But where Kant asks about a "what," Ignatius asks about a "who," the person of Jesus Christ, and our own relationship to that person, visualized as dying by that horrifying combination of torture and display, a crucifixion.

Ignatius seems convinced that to have a true sense of our personal sinfulness we need to have a deep sense of Christ crucified. A heightened awareness of sin should bring a heightened awareness of Christ dying for us on a cross.

THE SECOND, THIRD, AND FOURTH EXERCISES

In its first two points, the Second Exercise prescribed for the start of the Second Week asks the exercitant to recall their story of sin. Then they are to reflect on "the intrinsic foulness and malice of each "capital [deadly] sin committed, quite apart from its being forbidden" (SpEx 57). This theme had already surfaced in the very first annotation, where Ignatius maintained that "the divine will" seeks nothing else than "the good of the soul" (SpEx 1). In his *Summa Contra Gentiles* (3.122), Thomas Aquinas had classically expressed the way in which sinful offenses against God always harm our real good: "For we offend God only when we act against our own good" (*non enim Deus a nobis offenditur, nisi ex eo quo contra nostrum bonum agimus*).

Two comparisons should enter this meditation on my personal sins. I am asked to compare myself with all human beings, with all the angels and saints, and with the whole of creation. The aim is not merely to compare my own smallness with the greatness of all that reality. I should acknowledge my body to be full of "corruption and foulness," and "look at myself as though I were an ulcer or an abscess, the source of many sins and evils, and of great infection" (SpEx 58). When we read this today, we seem to be invited to enter the macabre imagery of Hieronymus Bosch (d. 1516) or at least the worst of scenes from the COVID-19 pandemic.

It is a relief when the meditation turns to compare the sinner's ignorance, weakness, injustice, and malice with God's wisdom, almighty power, justice, and goodness (SpEx 59). This comparison should issue in consoling, intensely felt "exclamations of wonder" that all created beings, including the earth, our common home, have let me live and keep me alive (SpEx 60).

In line with this consoling wonder, a deep sense of mercy dominates the brief colloquy: "all my thoughts will be about mercy, and I will thank God for giving me life up to now, proposing to do better in the future with his grace" (SpEx 61). Ignatius never tells the exercitant to ask directly for mercy, but only to open their minds and hearts to the divine mercy being offered.

The Third Exercise suggests a "repetition" of the First and Second Exercises, in particular dwelling upon the points at which the retreatants felt greater consolation and desolation or "greater spiritual relish" (SpEx 62). In Ignatius's experience, all spiritual situations, including desolation, offer creative and re-creative possibilities. In particular, he wants retreatants, when repeating previous exercises, to focus on the points that prompted deeper feeling and insight.

This exercise exemplifies his sense of the importance of reviewing (see SpEx 77) and repeating what has already happened at times of prayer. Ignatius saw little value in covering as much ground as possible (SpEx 76). Without citing it, he would have happily endorsed the Latin maxim, *non multa sed multum*, which one might translate roughly as "do not do many things but complete generously what you are about." This was a pillar of the spirituality spread by the late Michael Paul Gallagher.[5]

The Third Exercise concludes in a famous and effective way, with a triple colloquy (SpEx 63): first, with Our Lady, asking that she will obtain for me "from her Son and Lord three things":

"that I may feel an interior knowledge of my sins and an *abhorrence* for them";

"that I may feel a sense of the disorder in my actions, so that *abhorring* it I may amend my life and put order into it";

that I have a "knowledge of the world so that out of *abhorrence* for it I may put away from myself worldly and aimless things" (italics mine).

The colloquy is to end with a *Hail Mary*. Three times Ignatius uses *abhorrence*, implying a turning away (*aversio*) from sin, disorder, and worldly things, and a turning to God (*conversio ad Deum*).

After a passing mention of her (SpEx 47), this is the first serious engagement with the Blessed Virgin Mary in the Spiritual Exercises. It is first of many times Ignatius will refer to or prescribe the *Hail Mary*.

Retreatants are to enter a similar colloquy with the Son, asking that he obtain from the Father what they have already requested through the intercession of Mary. This second colloquy should end with the *Anima Christi*, a medieval prayer to Christ pervaded with references to his passion and death on the cross.

The triple colloquy ends with a direct approach to the Father and the same requests. It ends with the recitation of the *Our Father*.

THE FIFTH EXERCISE: MEDITATION ON HELL

Ignatius shared with medieval Christians (read Dante) and his contemporaries a firm belief that hell was a densely populated place. This belief, as it applied to innumerable non-Christians, fired the zeal of Ignatius's friend and fellow Jesuit, St. Francis Xavier, on his mission to the Far East. He was convinced that, by obeying the law of nature written in the hearts of all, "infidels" could be saved. Yet he believed that vast numbers of them went to hell and did so through their own fault.

For the Fifth Exercise of the First Week, Ignatius wanted the exercitants to ask that, "if through my faults I should ever forget the love of the Eternal Lord, at least the fear of punishment may help me not to fall into sin" (SpEx 65). At the very end of the Exercises, Ignatius explains that he is envisaging not so much servile fear or the fear of a slave but filial fear or the fear of a son (SpEx 370). Meditation on hell does not call into question the love of God, just as the situation of the prodigal son never leads him to question the father's love (Luke 15:11–24). In the meditation on hell, fear gives way to gratitude that God has not put "an end to my life. I should thank him for his constant loving kindness and mercy toward me right up to the present moment" (SpEx 71). While the fifteenth annotation speaks of God inflaming "the faithful soul" in "his love and praise," (SpEx 15), it is in the context of a meditation on hell that Ignatius speaks for the first time of the divine love in itself.

It is in the Second Week that Ignatius will explain for the first time the application of the five senses; he does so when he comes to the fifth contemplation of the Nativity of the Lord (SpEx 121). But the application of the senses is the method he proposes for the meditation on hell: imaginatively *seeing* the punishment suffered by the damned, *hearing* their cries, *smelling* the burning sulfur and the rotting matter, *tasting* bitter things, and *feeling* with the sense of touch "how those in hell are licked around and burned by the fires" (SpEx 66–70).

Ignatius did not speak here of applying the five senses, nor did Augustine when he wrote in his *Confessions* of the love of God:

> What is it that I love when I love you? Not the beauty of a body nor the glory of time, not the brilliance of light so pleasing to the eyes, not the sweet melodies of all kinds of songs, not the fragrance of flowers, ointments, and perfumes, not manna and honey; nor limbs that welcome the embrace of flesh. I do not love these when I love my God.
>
> And yet I love a kind of light, a kind of voice, a kind of fragrance, a kind of food, and a kind of embrace when I love my God, who is light, voice, fragrance, food, and the embrace of my inner person.
>
> There shines into my soul that which no place can hold; there sounds forth that which time cannot snatch away; and there is a fragrance that no breeze can disperse, a taste that eating does not diminish, and a clinging together that never loses its satisfaction. It is this that I love when I love my God. (10.6; trans. mine)

Hell means the absence of all such experience of God's love known through our interior senses. Ignatius, when inviting the retreatants to consider the eternal damnation of others and not the possible damnation of ourselves, brings into play the same five senses.

Both for the directors and exercitants, in a world in which hell is probably the last thing that they ever pray and think about, the meditation on hell can prove the most difficult. What composition of place should occupy their imagination? The situation of the prodigal son in a far country could be pressed into service to imagine his situation of emptiness and loneliness as hopeless and eternal. Or the exercitants might turn for images to the gas chambers of Auschwitz, war-torn areas of the Middle East and Ukraine, or camps of refugees and asylum seekers everywhere.

Followers and friends of Ignatius should be grateful that he does not display any sympathy with that gloating over the fate of the damned that many Christians in the past and some at least today have indulged. Take, for instance, the second-century Tertullian: "How shall I admire, how laugh, how exult, when I behold the many proud monarchs groaning in the lower abyss of darkness; so many magistrates liquefying in fiercer flames than they ever kindled against Christians; so many sage philosophers blushing in red-hot fires with their dilated pupils" (*De Spectaculis*, 30; my translation).

Jesus himself uttered dramatic warnings about the danger of being damned for eternity, notably in what was said to "those on the left" in the judgment of the nations: "Depart from me, you cursed, into the everlasting fire which has been prepared for the devil and his angels" (Matt 25:41; my translation). Nevertheless, in the late twentieth century, Hans Urs von Balthasar and Pope St. John Paul II, while not denying the real possibility of eternal damnation, encouraged Christians to hope and pray that there are no people actually in hell.[6] We hear something similar from Johann Sebastian Bach. At the end of his *St. Matthew Passion*, despite the words of Jesus about the traitor ("better for that man that he should not have been born," Matt 26:24; my translation), Bach calls Judas "*du verlorene Sohn* (you lost son)"—that is to say, the prodigal son who will be saved through the father's love. Do the prayers and hopes of von Balthasar and Pope John Paul II, not to mention Bach, finish evacuating hell of meaning or at least encourage people to ignore hell in their relationship with God?

It is essential to recall the nature of apocalyptic warnings in Jewish speech. The prophecy that Nineveh would be destroyed in forty days (Jonah 3:4) was not fulfilled. Through God's mercy the inhabitants of that large city repented of their sins, and they were spared destruction. Such warnings are always serious moral warnings but not necessarily predictions that literally come about.

What Jesus repeatedly stressed was the mysterious uncertainty of the final *Kairos*. He encouraged being constantly alert and faithfully doing the will of our loving Father.

DEATH AND SIN

More than any other part of the Exercises, the First Week raises the question: Should the directors propose material that is not contained explicitly in the text? While respecting the intentions of Ignatius, may the directors adapt his material? This is not a question about possibly abandoning the colloquy with Jesus on the cross (First Exercise) and the triple colloquy (Third and Fourth Exercise). Their extraordinary effectiveness makes them nonnegotiable items presented during the Spiritual Exercises.

Death

A good case can be made for substituting a meditation on death for the meditation on hell and for seriously updating the reflections on sin. Death does make a fleeting appearance in the First Exercise of the First Week, where the composition of place visualizes a body that will one day "disintegrate" (SpEx 47). Even more significantly, the sixth addition prescribes for the First Week thinking "more of death and judgment" (SpEx 78). We forget at our peril the Lord's parable of the rich fool (Luke 12:16–21).

Where the parable of the watchful servants encouraged the community expectation of the Lord's final coming (Luke 12:35–38), the parable of the rich fool shifts the focus to an individual. We are on common ground with Ignatius's individual meditating on hell. Like that individual, the rich man should not fail to recognize that he holds his life and wealth on loan from God. It does not occur to him to praise and thank God for all the abundant blessings he has received. Rather he sets about planning his future in a completely self-sufficient way.[7]

Visitors to the church of Santa Maria Novella in Florence will not easily forget the words at the foot of Masaccio's masterly portrayal of the crucifixion. A skeleton tells the viewer, "What you are I once was. What I am you one day will be." It is ultimate folly to forget our mortality. The parable of the rich fool recalls our common destiny, death; we are profoundly foolish if we dismiss it from our mind and thoughts. Our life is on loan from God. Both here and hereafter our existence comes from God and is owed to God. Our human story will be closed by death, a solitary, mysterious event, however it happens.

At the funeral Mass for Pope John Paul II in April 2005 and its concluding rites, there were numerous touching moments. For many of us present, the most moving episode came right at the end, after the coffin bearers lifted the simple, wooden casket from the ground in front of the altar. They carried John Paul II slowly and solemnly along the rows of presidents, monarchs, princes, prime ministers, and other powerful political leaders of our world. As he was borne past all those celebrities who enjoy lives of pomp and circumstance, it was as if the late pope were preaching his last sermon to them and saying, "You are all mortal. You too must face death and go home to God."

Sin

Before introducing some further material on sin, I think three things should be said to rehabilitate, if need be, the story of Adam and Eve. First, there is something very modern about the way our first parents excuse themselves. It almost seems that Adam blames God when saying, "The woman whom you gave to be with me, she gave me from the tree and I ate." When God confronts the woman, she too excuses herself: "The serpent tricked me and I ate" (Gen 3:12–13). Others are to blame; mistakes were made but not by me.[8]

Second, Ignatius notes how Adam and Eve initiate "the corruption that came upon the human race" (SpEx 51). Their sin turns them and their descendants into perpetrators of evil: in their dysfunctional family, one son (Cain) murders another (Abel). This leads to an expansion of violence (Gen 4:23–24) followed by a sinful breach of the divine-human boundaries (Gen 6:1–4). Seeing how "the wickedness of humankind was great," God decides on the great flood and a new creation of the world. The ancient myths of Genesis confirm Ignatius's sense of sin multiplying and sinners becoming perpetrators of ever greater evil.

But third, the old myths also confirm Ignatius's sense of God's loving care for sinners. Adam and Eve may have been driven out of the Garden of Eden, yet God cares for them by making garments for them (Gen 3:21). God cares also for the first murderer, by putting a mark upon Cain, "so that no one who came upon him would kill him" (Gen 4:15).

In Ignatius's meditations on sin, many have missed any direct connection with such sins of *omission* as those committed by the priest and the Levite in the story of the Good Samaritan (Luke 10:25–37), by those condemned at the last judgment for failure to help others (Matt 25:31–46), and by the rich man who fails to feed a starving Lazarus (Luke 16:19–31).[9] Jesus explicitly links the second and third story with the themes of death and judgment, which admirably suits the context of the First Week of the Exercises.

A few people think that the Exercises privatize sin or at least individualize sin. This might create problems for introducing such stories of individual sinners as the prodigal son and his elder brother (Luke 15:11–32) and King David's sins of adultery and murder (2 Sam 11:1–27). A growing awareness of the reality and significance of structural sin and our solidarity in such sin may exacerbate this difficulty. Consumers can be complicit in exploitative, unjust structures, along with directors, shareholders, and employees. Since we are beneficiaries of sinful structures and systems, do we need to repent of that?

Nevertheless, in many ways Jesus also authorizes and encourages individuals to reflect on their sins, and not least by telling the story of the prodigal son. Before the young man finds his way home to his father, he needs to "come to himself" (Luke 15:17). Jesus does not deal exclusively and collectively with "an evil generation that seeks signs" (Luke 11:29). To say the least, he leaves ample space for individuals to engage themselves with Ignatius's project of facing up to their disordered attachments and seeking and finding the divine will regarding the disposition of their lives (SpEx 1). Inevitably a concentration on the individual follows, right from the First Week's meditations on sin and hell. The texts constantly speak of "I," "me," and "my."

To conclude: I understand the scope of the First Week to recognize and accept myself as sinful and yet unconditionally loved by God. This acceptance enables us to rise gratefully above any fear, self-loathing, and feeling of being lost and ashamed. We can picture the situation as our enjoying the kind of acceptance we received as infants, that maternal love that is the paradigm of unconditional love.[10]

Ignatius, I believe, would agree with Liz Dodd when she wrote in the London *Tablet* on August 7, 2021, "Shame doesn't change hearts: only love can do that."

SECOND WEEK

5

THE CALL OF THE KING AND THE INCARNATION

God is called "king" fairly frequently in the Old Testament, but only once in the New Testament, when Jesus speaks of Jerusalem as "the city of the great King" (Matt 5:35). Jesus preached "the kingdom of God" but did not preach either God or himself as king. Typically Jesus named God as "Abba" ("Father dear") and himself as "the Son of Man." Nevertheless, Jesus is named "king" thirty-eight times in the New Testament and even "king of kings" in Revelation 17:14. All four Gospels state that the cross on which Jesus died carried the charge on which he was condemned: he had falsely claimed to "be king of the Jews."

Kingly words from Psalm 110 proved particularly important for the first Christians: "The LORD said to my Lord, 'Sit at my right hand, until I put your enemies under your feet.'" The New Testament echoes or quotes this verse twenty-one times, showing how significant it was for the emerging Church. The verse suggested that the risen Jesus shared in God's sovereign power over all things. He sits not under the throne of God nor simply near the throne of God. He sits on the divine throne, at the very right hand of God. In response, we can only pray, "Jesus is Lord; Jesus is King; Jesus is our everything."

It is a kingly parable that Ignatius proposes as the first exercise on a day of transition to the Second Week (SpEx 91–99). It will be followed by a contemplation on the incarnation. We consider first "the *call* of the earthly king," which "will help to contemplate the *life* of the eternal king" (SpEx 91; italics mine).

THE CALL OF THE EARTHLY KING

The composition of place for contemplating this call features "the synagogues, towns and villages" where Jesus went preaching. At least in that exercise of the imagination, he is not described as gathering an army, preparing for battle, and making war. The retreatants ask for the grace not to be deaf to the Lord's call but to be alert to fulfill his most holy will to the best of their ability (SpEx 91), desiring, significantly, to respond "in a spirit of love" (SpEx 97).

This low-key prayer is to be made only twice (SpEx 99), unlike the subsequent meditation on the two standards, "one [standard] that of Christ our Commander-in-Chief" and "the other that of Lucifer, the deadly enemy of our human nature, which is to be made four times" (SpEx 148).

Language also sets apart the call of the king. Without being presented as either a meditation or a contemplation, it invites the retreatants to "*consider* what reply good subjects should make to such an open and kindly king" (SpEx 94; italics mine). Earlier Ignatius had occasionally asked the retreatants to "consider" something (SpEx 59 and 77); in the call of the king he uses "consider" three times (SpEx 94, 95, and 96). Subsequently the invitation to "consider" seems to occur only once (SpEx 106).

Unlike the contemplations that follow (SpEx 106–7, 115, and 122–25, for example), Ignatius makes no reference to drawing "some profit" from the points for prayer. While the parable of "the call" opens in the normal way with a preparatory prayer and two preambles (SpEx 91), it differs from other exercises in that we find at its end neither an *Our Father* nor a colloquy. A final colloquy might have shown the trend and movement of the whole exercise. Instead, it ends by recommending an offering distinguished for "greater and more important sacrifices" (SpEx 96–98).

One must say that the *call* of the king dominates, rather than any *response* coming from others. The retreatants tend to remain spectators, rather than becoming one of the responsive group of "all you [who] have judgement and reason," that is to say, "those who want to respond in a spirit of love and to distinguish themselves" (SpEx 96, 97). We might have expected that the exercitants would have been asked more directly to offer themselves. A certain distance is maintained. In the contemplations that follow, the present tense is always used, and those making the Exercises naturally become part of the story (as in SpEx 116). Here, however, the composition of place (Christ "went preaching") treats events as remembered from the past (SpEx 91).

The imagery of kingship and serving a king had turned up in the First Week. There Ignatius pictures "a knight coming before his king and all the court, full of shame and confusion on account of offences committed against the lord from whom in the past he has had many gifts and favors" (SpEx 74). This generous lord foreshadows the "open and kindly king" of the Second Week. Anyone who refuses the request of such a king "would deserve to be blamed by everyone and to be judged an unworthy knight" (SpEx 94). Being an unworthy knight is certainly not admirable, even when it does not involve offenses committed against a lord who has been very generous with gifts and favors.

Ignatius himself had held a vigil of arms in Monserrat on the eve of the Annunciation in 1522; he wished to express a complete break with his previous life.[1] During his months at nearby Manresa, he was not thinking of warfare and conquests, spiritual or otherwise, but of going to the Holy Land and spending the rest of his life there. Warlike terminology does not appear in his letters, the constitutions, or spiritual diary. In his "Reminiscences" or autobiography, Ignatius once calls himself *nuevo soldato de Cristo* (a new soldier of Christ),[2] but around eighty times he presents himself as "the pilgrim."

In the text of the Spiritual Exercises the terminology of war has only a limited place. The call of "the earthly king" speaks of "conquering all the land of the infidels"—an obvious reference to the Christian Crusades against nonbelievers—and the coming "victory." But the king speaks more of food and drink, clothing, working by day and watching by night, and sharing in "labors" (SpEx 93).

When the call goes out from Christ "the eternal king," Ignatius is engaged with explaining his parable of "the earthly king" and the language moves closer to the Gospels. While the eternal king's "will...to conquer the whole world and every enemy," this aims at "entering into the *glory* of my Father." Hence all "who want to come with me will have to labor with me, so that by following me in my *suffering*, they may also follow me into my *glory*" (SpEx 95; italics mine). Ignatius echoes here Luke 24:26: "Did not the Christ have to suffer these things and enter into his glory?" "Come with me" and "follow me" echo, of course, the Gospel accounts of the calling of the first disciples.

Nevertheless, some of this language jars with that of the Gospels. Conquering "the whole world and every enemy" conflicts with the command of Jesus: "Love your enemies, pray for those who persecute you" (Matt 5:44). There is a hint of elitist spirituality when Ignatius observes that those who want "to distinguish themselves by the thoroughness of their commitment" to the "eternal King and universal Lord" will "offer greater and more important sacrifices" (SpEx 97). Far from preaching an elitist spirituality, Jesus calls *all his followers* to "be perfect" as their "heavenly Father is perfect" (Matt 5:48).

All in all, the militaristic language, which abounds in many books of Sacred Scripture right through to the Book of Revelation and then shapes innumerable Christian hymns,[3] remains limited in the Spiritual Exercises and sometimes confined to "the enemy of our human nature" (SpEx 327). Even the phrase *sub crucis vexillo militari* (to be a solder under the standard of the cross), which is found in the earliest descriptions and approbations of the Society of Jesus,[4] is not found in the meditation of the Two Standards.

Nevertheless, a military reading of the Spiritual Exercises and of Jesuit life entered the tradition, a development that was reflected spectacularly in the twentieth century by Arthur Vermeersch's *Miles Christi Iesu*.[5] In an unintentionally comic 1988 thriller set in Rome, *Russicum*, F. Murray Abraham plays the role of the Jesuit rector of the Russicum (the Russian College opposite the Basilica of St. Mary Major). This unfortunate actor, who had starred as Salieri in *Amadeus* and won an Oscar and Golden Globe for his performance, was now condemned to mouthing such inaccurate platitudes encouraged by Vermeersch and a long-standing tradition: "I am a soldier of Christ."

Before leaving the call of the Eternal King, we should not miss a second "note" that follows: "For the Second Week, as well as for the future, it is very helpful to read from time to time from the *Imitation of Christ*, the Gospels, or lives of the saints" (SpEx 100). Ignatius intends a prayerful reading of these texts. When prayerfully reading the Gospels (and the other inspired Scriptures), one is engaged in what has traditionally been called *lectio divina*. To explain the story and practice of *lectio divina*, I have added an appendix to this book. Doing the Spiritual Exercises could readily initiate an authentic Christian life nourished by the regular practice of *lectio divina*, which involves quietly mulling over not only the Gospels but also other books of the Sacred Scriptures.

THE CONTEMPLATION ON
THE INCARNATION

Combining the language of Paul about the coming of "the fullness of time" (Gal 4:4) with the story of the annunciation to Mary (Luke 1:26–38) (SpEx 102, 262), Ignatius pictures the three Divine Persons looking at the human race so much in danger of ending in hell (SpEx 102, 106, 108).[6] They decide that the Second Person would take on the human condition and save the human race. They send the angel Gabriel to Our Lady.

The Individual

This contemplation on the incarnation brings together the individual retreatant and the whole of humanity. The retreatant is invited to pray as follows: "I ask for interior knowledge of the Lord who became human for me, so that I may better love and follow him" (SpEx 104). Here Ignatius is the beneficiary of

---

a wonderful medieval tradition, best known through the prayer attributed to St. Richard of Chichester (d. 1253): "Thanks be to thee, my Lord Jesus Christ, for all the benefits thou hast given me, for all the pain and insult thou hast borne for me. O most merciful Redeemer, Friend, and Brother, may I know thee more clearly, love thee more dearly, and follow thee more nearly." This prayer, to be found at his tomb, moves effectively from calling Christ our "Redeemer" to naming him also "Friend" and even "Brother." In a lyric "Day by Day," the 1971 musical *Godspell* made known and popularized the closing words about knowing, loving, and following Jesus.

A concluding colloquy will address the three Divine Persons, or the Word incarnate, or his Mother—the choice being determined by "my inner feelings—so that I may better follow *and imitate* Our Lord, thus newly incarnate" (SpEx 109). Since the story of the incarnate Son of God has hardly begun, retreatants may be left wondering about the extent of their following him, now specified as imitating him. The rest of the Second Week will fill out an answer for them.

The language of the Exercises has decisively moved forward: from "follow" (SpEx 95) to "imitate" (SpEx 109). Imitating the Lord Jesus turns up in the oldest, extant Christian document (1 Thess 1:6) and is associated with imitating the apostle Paul himself (1 Cor 4:16; 11:1–2; 2 Thess 3:7). For Paul, the imitation of Christ means a deliverance from sin that conforms believers to the crucifixion and resurrection (Rom 6:1–11; Phil 3:10, 21), being shaped by the Holy Spirit (Rom 8:4, 11), and being committed in loving service to others (1 Cor 13:1–13; Gal 5:13).

A World Outlook

At the incarnation, which will make possible the following and imitation of Christ, the three Divine Persons see various kinds of people "on the face of the earth, some white and some black, some in peace and others at war, some weeping and some laughing, some healthy, others sick, some being born and others dying," and so forth (SpEx 106). The retreatants are also invited to "hear what the people on the face of the earth talk about," as well as hearing what the Divine Persons speak about ("let us bring about the redemption of the human race") and what Gabriel and the Blessed Virgin Mary talk about. Finally, in a limited application of the senses, the retreatants are to look again at what these various groups are doing (SpEx 107–08).

This presentation of the incarnation emphasizes a world outlook. It blatantly does so by attending in considerable detail to all that people are doing and suffering on the whole face of the earth. Little is said about Our Lady and nothing explicitly about the Holy Spirit, whose power will "overshadow" her in the incarnation.

Mary and the Holy Spirit

Directors might consider introducing some "narrative" from the encounter between Mary and Gabriel. Imitating Ignatius's use of a "point" system when presenting material, we can say: (1) Mary exemplifies supremely how human beings, by accepting a remarkable gift for themselves, receive it also for others. (2) Her hidden, Ignatius would say "humble," act in saying "yes" to the divine plan was the most decisive act toward the salvation of all creation performed by a "merely" human being. (3) Mary had never literally rehearsed the scene of the annunciation. Her holy and faithful life had been a perfect preparation for this moment. Mary's "yes" to God characterized her whole life before and after the annunciation.

Here and elsewhere the Holy Spirit, while clearly one of the three Divine Persons preeminently involved in the incarnation, is not called the "agent" of the incarnation as happens in Luke's Gospel ("the Holy Spirit will come upon you") and the Apostles' Creed ("conceived of the Holy Spirit"). The annunciation (SpEx 262) will lead off the pages when Ignatius gives points for meditating or contemplating the mysteries of Christ's life. But nothing is said about the Holy Spirit in what is a substantial summary of this initial mystery of the annunciation.

When listing the mysteries of Christ's life, Ignatius naturally includes the baptism of Christ. Here there is a briefest reference to the descent of the Holy Spirit (SpEx 273).

In what Ignatius names as the "fifth appearance" of the risen Christ (SpEx 304), namely, John 20:19–23, there will be an explicit mention of the Holy Spirit. In that encounter with the disciples, Jesus gifts them with the Holy Spirit. But the mysteries of Christ listed in the Spiritual Exercises end with the ascension (SpEx 312) and do not go on to include Pentecost.

This relative silence about the Holy Spirit may seem unexpected by those who have read Ignatius's "Reminiscences." There he recalls not only a mystical vision of the Holy Trinity but also his habit of praying "each day to the three persons separately."[7] The Exercises contain abundant prayer to the God the Father and the Son, but very little prayer addressed to the Holy Spirit.

A CODA: SØREN KIERKEGAARD, "THE KING AND THE MAIDEN"[8]

In a parable that, as he admits, sounds like a fairy tale, Kierkegaard imagines a maiden who belongs to the poorest class and lives in the most deprived circumstances. A powerful and noble-minded king falls in love with her. He is troubled by the questions: "Would she be happy to live at his side? Could she summon up enough courage never to remember what the king would wish only to forget: that he is king and she has been a humble maiden?" "Even if," Kierkegaard continues, "the maiden would be content to become as nothing, this could not satisfy the king, precisely because he loves her, and because it is harder for him to be her benefactor than to lose her."

Kierkegaard applies his parable to God, who is driven by love to reveal himself and to "win" the human "learner." In and through love "the unequal can be made equal"; and in and through this "equality or unity...an understanding can be effected." But, without "annihilating the unlikeness that exists between them," how is God going to overcome the infinite difference and "make himself understood"?

Or, to return to the king, how could the love between the king and the maiden be a truly happy love without any deception or delusion entering in? It would be terrible deception, Kierkegaard observes, to "elevate" abruptly the humble maiden and let her suddenly find her "fortune made." The "tumultuous joy" of such an outward change would deceive the king's own heart and the maiden herself. Or the king might "show himself to the humble maiden in all the pomp of his power, causing the sun of his presence to rise over her cottage, shedding a glory over the scene, and making her forget herself in worshipful admiration." This might "satisfy the maiden, but it would not satisfy the king." After all, he desires "not his glorification but hers." He cannot deceive her; to express imperfectly his love for her would be "in his eyes a deception." Union, Kierkegaard concludes, "must be attempted by a descent."

The parable thus reaches this point: for union to be brought about, love must "alter itself." God must become our equal and "appear in the likeness of the humblest" and "in the form of a servant." Both for God and for the king, "the unfathomable nature of love...desires equality with the beloved." In God's case omnipotent love can accomplish its purpose—something the king could not do. His "beggar-cloak" will "flutter loosely about him" and betray him. In the case of the incarnate Son of God, his "servant-form is no mere outer garment." He "must suffer all things, endure all things, make experience of all things. He must suffer hunger in the desert, he must thirst in the time of his agony, he must be forsaken in death."

Kierkegaard's answer to the question: "What did the incarnation do to God?" echoes, of course, what St. Paul wrote in Philippians 2:8–11 about Jesus Christ, who, "being first in the form of God, took the form of a servant" and "emptied himself" in his incarnation. The One who "did not think his being equal to God something to be exploited" to his own advantage became human and "obedient to death, even death on a cross." The apostle Paul underlines here the terrifying contrast between the state of "being equal to God" and "dying on a cross."

6

THE BIRTH OF CHRIST AND THE SHADOW OF THE CROSS

Beyond question, Ignatius valued highly what retreatants could draw from contemplating the birth of Jesus and related "mysteries" (such as the Presentation in the Temple and the Flight into Egypt) (SpEx 110–34). Toward the end of the Spiritual Exercises Ignatius uses his system of three points when providing a full list of such mysteries: from the Annunciation to Mary through to the twelve-year-old Christ remaining in the Jerusalem temple (SpEx 263–72).

Ignatius's repeated invitation to pray over the nativity by applying our senses (SpEx 121–26, 129, 132–33) respects the way the birth of every child, and uniquely the birth of *this* Child, "fills up" our senses, albeit not quite as John Denver meant in his 1973 "Annie's Song." This chapter will first respond to that invitation and then offer points for prayer about two groups closely connected with the birth of Jesus, the shepherds (SpEx 265) and the Magi (SpEx 267). It will conclude with a lengthy reflection on how "Christ comes to be born in extreme poverty and, after so many labors, after hunger, thirst, heat and cold, outrages and affronts, he dies on the cross, and all of this for me" (SpEx 116).

APPLICATION OF THE
SENSES TO THE NATIVITY

Contemplating the incarnation on the First Day of the Second Week, the retreatants ask "for an interior knowledge of the Lord who became human for me, so that I may better love and follow him" (SpEx 104). Nevertheless, Ignatius then speaks at times, less specifically, of drawing or deriving "some profit" from the prayer (SpEx 122–25). As always, he respects the freedom of God's dealings with the retreatants. They may experience their prayer as "profitable," but not exactly as yielding an "interior knowledge of the Lord."

In our application of the senses (SpEx 121–26), the mind's eye should "*see* the persons," above all the Christ Child. We should also *hear* "what the persons say or could say." Here I would like to add: "we hear the cries of the Child." If the Christ Child did not sometimes cry, that raises a question about the historical truth of a genuine incarnation.

Ignatius asks us to "*smell* and *taste* the infinite gentleness and sweetness of the divinity, and of the soul and of its virtues." In the words of the Psalmist, "taste and see the goodness of the Lord" (Ps 34:8). But what of smelling the fragrance of the tiny Baby after it had been washed? And, for that matter, if he was born in a stable, what about the various odors connected with animals, including the ox and the donkey (SpEx 111) that Ignatius pictures as going to Bethlehem with Mary and Joseph?

Finally, Ignatius honors the sense of touch: we "embrace and kiss the places where these persons (the member of the Holy Family) tread and sit." What of our embracing and kissing the Christ Child himself? Among Spaniards and those of Spanish descent, many still lift up and kiss a doll representing the newborn Jesus among the figures in the Christmas Crib. Sensitivities differ, but at least some retreatants will want to "apply their senses" by picking up the Christ Child and embracing him.

THE SHEPHERDS AND THE MAGI

After proposing for contemplation the nativity of Christ, Ignatius makes room for the shepherds and Magi who visited Bethlehem. They can profitably focus prayer at this stage of the Exercises.

(1) Economically the shepherds rate nowhere near the Magi; the only gift they bring is themselves. (2) Religiously, the shepherds may be on the fringe of Jewish society, but, unlike the Magi, they are not Gentile outsiders. (3) A short walk brings the shepherds to the Christ; the Magi had to travel a considerable distance.

(1) Both the shepherds and the Magi are disadvantaged and need help. The shepherds need an angel of the Lord, backed up by a heavenly army, "a multitude of heavenly soldiers" (William Tyndale), to stir them into heading for Bethlehem. The Magi do not know the biblical prophecies; they have the benefit only of the star. (2) The priests and scribes know the Scriptures (above all, the prophecy of Micah about the Messiah being born in Bethlehem), but they do not join the Magi and go a few miles to Bethlehem. Those with decisive advantages can fail to make use of them. (3) Contemplate the shepherds and the Magi in the Christmas cribs or on Christmas cards.

THE NATIVITY IN VIEW OF
THE CROSS AND RESURRECTION

In his commentary on the Gospel of Luke, François Bovon discusses the Roman census that brings Mary and Joseph to Bethlehem for the birth of Jesus (Luke 2:1–5). He draws attention to "the striking juxtaposition of [a] the emperor [Augustus, the ruler of the *imperium romanum*, which covered the *oikumenē* or inhabited world] known to all, with [b] the hidden Messiah."[1] In the contemplation on the nativity, Ignatius hints at this juxtaposition. He mentions "the tribute which Caesar had imposed" (SpEx 111) and eventually describes it in terms of "Joseph acknowledging his subjection to Caesar" (SpEx 264).

Elsewhere Ignatius alerts retreatants to the humility that Christ showed and the humiliations he suffered. In the meditation on the Two Standards, he will imagine Christ our Lord, "the supreme and true commander," taking "his stand in a lowly place" (SpEx 143–44). Before proposing the Elections, Ignatius wants retreatants "to consider attentively" three kinds of humility, the third of which incorporates imitating Christ in his poverty and in "ignominy rather than fame" (SpEx 164, 167). For the contemplation on the nativity, Ignatius might have contrasted the humility and anonymity of Christ, born "in a lowly place," with the "fame" and earthly power of Augustus ruling his empire from his Roman palace. But it is a cross that takes the form of "extreme poverty" highlighted by Ignatius.

The Extreme Poverty of the Nativity

For the contemplation on the nativity, Ignatius proposes considering what they (Mary, Joseph, and a servant girl) are doing: "their travel and efforts, so that Christ comes to be born in extreme poverty and, after so many labors, after hunger, thirst, heat and cold, outrages and affronts, he dies on the cross" (SpEx 116). In his notes for "the mysteries of the life of Christ our Lord," Ignatius adds details from Luke 2:7: "She [Mary] bore her first-born son, and wrapped him in clothes, and placed him in the manger, [because there was no room for them in the inn]" (SpEx 264).

Summing up the circumstances of Jesus' birth as those of "extreme poverty," Ignatius anticipates the suffering that would ensue when Jesus grew to manhood: a ministry, characterized by "so many labors, hunger, thirst, heat and cold," the passion when Jesus faced "outrages and affronts," and, finally, death "on the cross." Being placed after birth in a feeding trough for animals is not the only detail explicitly cited to explain what constituted the extreme poverty that opened a life of suffering that would end with crucifixion.

In the composition of place for contemplating the nativity, Ignatius speaks of "the grotto" in which Jesus was born (SpEx 112). "Since there was no place for them in the inn [*kataluma*]" (Luke 2:7), Jesus was born in a grotto or cave. Here Ignatius follows an early tradition about Jesus being born in a cave, which was derived from the *Protoevangelium of James* (18.1) and St. Justin Martyr (*Dialogue with Trypho*, 78) in the second century, and Origen (*Contra Celsum*, 1.51) in the third century. On his own pilgrimage to the Holy Land, the cave of the nativity could have been one of the shrines Ignatius visited, even if he does not explicitly mention this.[2]

Modern biblical scholarship supports Ignatius's notion of "extreme poverty" through the various translations it endorses for "manger (*phatnē*)." While it probably means (a) a feeding trough for animals,[3] it could also mean (b) an indoor or outdoor "stable" or "stall" where animals were tied up or penned (as in Luke 13:15), or (c) "a feeding place under the open sky, in contrast to *kataluma*, a shelter where people stayed."[4] Any of these three meanings indicates the extreme poverty that characterized the place where Mary and Joseph stopped and where Jesus was born. He came into this world, not in a proper shelter for human beings nor in a proper place for a birth, but among the animals.

The text of Ignatius does not incorporate literally the early tradition of animals being present around the manger, a tradition inspired by words of Isaiah 1:3[5] and incorporated in the practice of Christmas cribs launched by St Francis of Assisi (d. 1226). But Ignatius has already included, in the first preamble to the contemplation on the nativity, a donkey on which Mary rides from Nazareth to Bethlehem and an ox that Joseph and a servant girl bring along as well. Two animals have shared the journey from Nazareth and are thought to be present to share also in the birth at Bethlehem (SpEx 111).

One modern interpretation of *phatnē* connects it with the entombment of Jesus. When born, he was placed in a manger, just as after his crucifixion he would be placed in a tomb (Luke 23:53).[6] This view unintentionally coincides with icons of the nativity created by Eastern Christians. They portray the newly born Christ Child wrapped in what might pass as a shroud and lying in a kind of trough that has been cut in a large rock and could seem like a tiny tomb.

In Luke's nativity narrative, the swaddling clothes symbolize the ordinary, human condition of the newborn Christ Child.

Like any baby he was wrapped in bands of cloth (see Wis 7:4–7). Mary "did for Jesus what any ancient Palestinian mother would have done for a newborn babe." What she did expressed her "maternal care."[7]

Some Western artists link the swaddling clothes of the Christ Child with the loin cloth he will wear on the cross. Thus on the Isenheimer altar painted by Matthias Grünewald (d. 1528), "in his portrayal of Christmas, Our Lady holds her child in the same cloth that Jesus will wear at the end of his life on the cross."[8] Sometimes, as in the case of Sandro Botticelli's "The Mystical Nativity" (see below), the swaddling clothes are associated with the shroud in which he will be buried.

Geertgen Tot Sint Jans (d. about 1490) does not make either of these links; he omits the swaddling clothes altogether. In his *The Nativity at Night*, found in the National Gallery, London, the Child lies completely naked in a rough, hard container, more a tomb than a cradle. Christ's future suffering can also be detected in the way Geertgen encloses the composition within the wooden beams of a stable. On the one hand, the beams show us that the Child, although naked, is protected by a roof. On the other hand, the way in which the beams extend into the sky hints at the wooden arms of the cross on which the Child will die for us.

Sacred art, both East and West, converges with Ignatius in linking the birth of Christ with his crucifixion. But we should not neglect the way Ignatius (and before him) Luke introduces elements of cross *and resurrection* in presenting the story of the nativity. Both Ignatius and Luke do this through the angels who encounter the shepherds and send them to Bethlehem. Luke *also* includes, as we shall see, elements of cross and resurrection through the three "inns" that punctuate his narrative: Luke 2:7; 10:34; and 22:11.

The Shepherds

In his *notes on the mysteries* of Christ's life, Ignatius quotes from Luke's Gospel 2:13–14 to propose the third point for prayer inspired by "the Nativity of Christ Our Lord": "There came a multitude of the heavenly army, which said, 'glory to God in the heavens'" (SpEx 264). Following straight on from the second point for the contemplation on the nativity ("she bore her first-born son, and wrapped him in clothes, and placed him in the manger"), the third point implies that "a multitude of the heavenly army" came to the place of Christ's birth and there proclaimed "glory to God in the heavens." From their appearing to shepherds out in the countryside, Ignatius has moved the multitude of angels into Bethlehem where they announce the glory of God revealed in the lowly birth of the Messiah. This does not correspond to Luke's narrative, in which the angels leave the shepherds and return "into heaven" (Luke 2:15). The "divine glory shines not around the manger but around the angels," appearing outside Bethlehem to shepherds. It is they alone who go into town and bear witness to a heavenly revelation (Bovon, vol. 1, 87).[9]

Ignatius belongs to a tradition, reflected in Christian art both before and after his time, that placed an angelic host proclaiming the nativity right there in the stable or grotto where Christ was born. This tradition, through the presence of angels in Bethlehem, associates heavenly glory, and not merely the cross, with the cave where Jesus was born and the manger in which he was laid. "The Mystical Nativity" (1500–1) by Botticelli (now in the National Gallery, London), portrays an open cave in which Jesus was born but includes twelve angels dancing under the golden dome of heaven right above the Child, who lies on a sheet in his rustic manger. For good measure, at the bottom of the painting three more angels embrace three men. Botticelli's masterpiece blends earthly poverty and lowliness with heavenly joy and celebration, the cross with the glory of risen life.

Ignatius's *notes* for a contemplation "on the shepherds" (Luke 2:8–20) immediately follow those for a contemplation of the nativity, and feature even more heavenly glory and corresponding human joy. According to the first point, "the nativity of Christ Our Lord is made known to the shepherds by the angel: 'I declare to you a great joy, because today the Savior of the world has been born.'" Ignatius closes his sketch for a contemplation on the shepherds with the third point: "the shepherds went back, glorifying and praising the Lord." The glory and joy of the resurrection pervade the first and third points. Poverty and the cross make their appearance in the second point. The shepherds "found the child laid in the manger" when they went to Bethlehem (SpEx 265).

In his contemporary biblical commentary, Bovon presents a vision of Jesus' birth that "intertwines glory and lowliness." A heavenly army of angels witnesses to the greatness of Jesus who is Savior and Christ the Lord; the manger expresses the lowliness of his birth. The "humble birth" "stands under the sign of the cross" (vol. 1, 93), conveyed specifically through the sign of the manger. Bovon notes "the thrice-repeated, refrain-like occurrence of 'child lying in a manger'" (vol. 1, 90). Mary "laid" her newborn son "in a manger" (Luke 2:7); the sign that the shepherds received from the angel of the Lord was that of "a child wrapped in bands of cloth and lying in a manger" (Luke 2:12); when the shepherds went to Bethlehem, they found "the child lying in a manger" (Luke 2:16). Heavenly glory was not absent but conveyed, specifically, through the angels.

Bovon uses two sermons by Martin Luther, a contemporary of Ignatius, to summarize the message of human misery and heavenly glory conveyed by the Lukan account of Jesus' birth. The Savior was born so wretchedly on earth, but there followed the happy song of the angels (Bovon, vol. 1, 93–94). The sign of the manger interpreted the birth of one who would die on a cross, but his birth was also the occasion of a revelation of divine glory (Luke 2:8–9) and of a heavenly liturgy led by an angelic choir (Luke 2:13–14). That revelation and liturgy acclaimed the "peace" that God conveys and the human "joy" it occasions (Luke 2:10, 14).

Bovon appropriately points to an *inclusio* that, through the presence of angels, binds together the humble "birth" of Christ and "his rebirth in the resurrection."[10] At the end angels will attest "the hand of God at work" in the resurrection (Luke 24:4), when "the people experience peace" (Luke 24:36) and "great joy" (Luke 24:52) (Bovon, vol. 1, 88). The *inclusio* joins cross and resurrection.

Three Inns as Scenes of Cross and Resurrection

Reflecting on the inn where Mary and Joseph found no room, Bovon notes how "the holy duty of hospitality" had waned since the days of tribal nomads (Bovon, vol. 1, 86). But the inn in Bethlehem is only the first of three inns in Luke's Gospel where such a place of hospitality is endowed with meaning drawn from the cross and resurrection.

Luke's story of Jesus' birth states that the baby was "laid in a manger, because there was no place for them in the inn (*kataluma*)" (Luke 2:7). The New Revised Standard Version (NRSV) translates *kataluma* as "inn," as do the Revised English Bible (REB) and the Jerusalem Bible (JB). The King James Version (KJV) had called it "the village inn," unlike its influential predecessor, the Tyndale Bible, which translated the verse as Mary "layed him in a manger because ther was no roume for them in the ynne." Suggesting that "inn" (Bovon, vol. 1, 80) is probably intended "vaguely," Bovon thinks of "a room in a private house in which travelers could usually spend the night." But he also speaks of a roadhouse, "a place where one can stop and unharness a mount or draught animal...a provisional place to spend the night" (Bovon, vol. 1, 86).

The noun *kataluma* has a related verb *kataluō* ("to let/bring down"). The meanings of this verb vary widely but include putting down one's baggage, unharnessing an animal, unloading its burden, stop doing what one is doing, and so halt, rest, find lodging (*kataluma*), and receive hospitality. We find the verb used with one or more of such meanings in Luke 9:12 and 19:7.

Almost halfway through Luke's Gospel, Jesus delivers his famous parable of the Good Samaritan (Luke 10:25–37). The Samaritan takes a wounded traveler to an "inn" (NRSV, REB, and JB), does his best for him, and leaves him next day in the care of the "innkeeper" (NRSV, REB, and JB). The two terms in Greek are, respectively, *pandocheion* and *pandocheus*; each term occurs only here in the entire New Testament. Etymology suggests their meaning: "*pan* [all] *docheion* [receiving]," that is, receiving/welcoming anyone and everyone who comes along.

Toward the end of Luke's Gospel, Jesus sends Peter and John into Jerusalem to prepare the Passover, where they are to say to the owner of a house: "the teacher asks you, 'where is the guest room [*kataluma*], where I may eat the Passover with my disciples?' He will show you a large room upstairs [*anagaion*], already furnished. Make preparations for us there" (Luke 22:8–12; NRSV). In this passage from Luke, the REB translates *kataluma* simply as "the room" rather than as "the guest room," and continues: "he [the householder] will show you a large room upstairs, all set out." The JB renders *kataluma* as "the dining room" and then, by inserting "with couches," adds to what we find in the Greek text: "the man will show you a large upper room furnished with couches."[11] It is only in Luke 2:7, 22:11, and Mark 14:14 (on which Luke 22:11 draws) that we find *kataluma* in the whole of the New Testament.

The magisterial *Greek-English Lexicon of the New Testament and Other Early Christian Literature* (BDAG) judges "inn" to be only a possible translation in Luke 2:7, with *kataluma* being "best understood" here as "lodging" or "guest-room" as in Luke 22:11.[12] The context of Luke 22:11 (and Mark 14:14) would also permit "the sense [of] dining room." *Pandocheion* (Luke 10:34) is the more specific term for "inn," where a traveler could find lodging.[13] Thus BDAG prefers "lodging" or "guest-room" for Luke 2:7, "inn" for Luke 10:34, and "lodging," "guestroom," or "dining room" for Luke 22:11.

So much for the translation of three passages from Luke. How might this use of *kataluma* (twice) and *pandocheion* (once) be drawn together and nourish reflection on the cross and resurrection? Jesus came into this world, not in a *kataluma*, which offered a normal stopping place where people on a journey could shelter, but in some kind of stable in which Mary placed her newborn child in a trough for feeding animals. That "there was no room for them in the inn" prompts prayerful thought about the presence of the cross right from the beginning of Jesus' story.[14] But we have also seen how this failure in hospitality was offset by the anticipation of resurrection conveyed by the heavenly glory and angelic message revealed to the shepherds. We find life, even heavenly life, as well as death, in contemplating the story of Jesus' nativity.

The Inn of the Good Samaritan

In Luke's Gospel after the nativity story, we hear no more of Bethlehem or mangers. But an inn (*pandocheion*) returns with the parable of the Good Samaritan (Luke 10:29–37). Even before that, the verb which corresponds to *kataluma* has turned up. At the end of a day on which Jesus had spoken in a deserted place to a crowd of five thousand "about the kingdom of God" and "healed those who needed to be cured," the twelve apostles came to him and said: "Send this crowd away, so that they may go into the surrounding villages and countryside, to find lodging [*katalusōsin*] and get provisions." Instead, Jesus multiplied five loaves and two fish and fed the crowd (Luke 9:11–17). The apostles had presumed that, late in the day and even for such a large number of people, lodging and food would be available elsewhere.

Despite the differences between the miraculous feeding (concerning the needs of thousands) and a story involving only a handful of people, an "example story,"[15] as some call the parable of the Good Samaritan, a similar presumption shows up. The Samaritan seems to take it for granted that he will find shelter and care for a wounded man at a nearby "inn."

Unlike some parables that may feature only one or two characters—for instance, the sower and the seeds (Luke 8:4–15) and the lost sheep (Luke 15:3–7)—the parable of the Good Samaritan includes several dramatis personae: the man traveling to Jericho, the robbers, a priest, a Levite, a Samaritan, and an innkeeper. The hero who practices compassion toward someone in dreadful need is undoubtedly the Samaritan, described by Bovon as "a nondescript individual with a despised background," someone "usually associated with evil" (Bovon, vol. 2, 56, 57). The Samaritan's heart goes out to the wounded traveler. Through administering first aid and transporting him to a nearby inn, he establishes a "relationship" with him (Bovon, vol. 2, 58). "Having done his part, the Samaritan passed the torch to others"—in particular, to the innkeeper. He has "taken care" of the wounded man and asks the innkeeper to do the same (Bovon, vol. 2, 59).

It is the example of the Samaritan that provides the central answer to the question: "Who is my neighbor?" (Luke 10:29). But what of the innkeeper? Does his heart go out to the wounded traveler? We do not know, but we do know that he establishes a relationship with the man by agreeing at once to give him shelter and care. He does not object: "There is no room for badly wounded people in my inn." To be sure, he is given two denarii by the Samaritan, who promises that, on his return, he will repay any further expenses. The innkeeper does not supply lodging and help for nothing. But he lives up to the meaning of his name in Greek, someone who "receives everyone." His kind help may be less spectacular, but it does carry further the concern and care of the Good Samaritan. The innkeeper is also a true neighbor to someone in great distress. If this example story invites its readers to "be a Good Samaritan," it also invites them, albeit secondarily, to "be a Good Innkeeper."

Ancient Christianity provides examples of writers positively appreciating the inn and the innkeeper, and not merely the Good Samaritan. Bovon summarizes Origen's account of an earlier interpretation that understood the innkeeper to be "the head of the Church, in charge of administration." Bovon goes on to quote from Origen's *Homilies on Luke*, 34.7: "The Samaritan...carries the dying man and takes him to an inn, that is, into the Church that welcomes everyone, does not refuse aid to anyone, and to which all are invited by Jesus" (Bovon, vol. 2, 60–61).

Bovon notes how "in the past the image of the Samaritan was often applied to Christ giving help to humanity, rather than to some charitable Christian."[16] Bovon has no quarrel with this christological application, provided that it is not "done at the expense of the ethical dimension." He explains: the "Christological structure is rooted in God, who is compassionate and active, and acts through the Church, whose members carry on their Lord's charitable acts by means of their faith and practice" (Bovon, vol. 2, 51).

Bovon also recalls how "Samaritan" in Hebrew means "watchman" or "shepherd" (Bovon, vol. 2, 58 n38). Being a Good

Samaritan hints at the Good/Beautiful Shepherd, who lays down his life for his sheep (see John 10:11, 14).

Cross and resurrection belong to the example story that Jesus told, in the sense that it turned on a traveler in great distress. He had been robbed, beaten, and left half dead, only to be rescued and nursed back to life in the shelter of an inn. But we should not ignore the personal loss and personal risk suffered by the Good Samaritan. His kindness cost him some oil, wine, clothing, and money—as well as the loss of time caused by an unforeseen break in his journey. We should also remember the element of danger: if one traveler had been robbed, bandits could still have been prowling around to attack and rob others. It was dangerous to stop at the side of the road and then move slowly ahead keeping a gravely wounded man from falling off his seat on the pack animal.

The life of Jesus, as Christian preachers and others have appreciated, dramatized his role as the Good Samaritan (Bovon, vol. 2, 64 n75). Luke encouraged them to do so by providing a link through a striking verb, "his heart went out [*esplanchnisthē*]," with which he described not only the reaction of Jesus to the widow of Nain who had just lost her only son (Luke 7:13) but also the reaction of the Samaritan (Luke 10:33) to the half-dead traveler. At his own personal risk and cost, Jesus stopped to save wounded people who had been robbed and stripped. But in this case, however, compassionate love for his neighbors cost much more than possessions, money, and time. Jesus as the good Samaritan was stripped and wounded in his passion. He became the Victimized Traveler, not rescued but left to die on a cross.

To conclude, the parable of the Good Samaritan reflects its lights and shadows back over the earlier story of Christ's nativity. It does so not only (a) through the contrast between two inns, the first in which there was "no room" for the birth of the messianic shepherd (prophesied by Micah 5:2–5a) and the second in which a wounded traveler found unquestioning shelter and care, but also (b) through the figures of the Good Samaritan (or Good Shepherd) and the Good Innkeeper. The cross and the resurrection belong in both the parable and the story of the nativity.

The "Inn" of the Last Supper

Before we arrive at the *kataluma* where Jesus celebrated the Passover with his disciples on the night before he died (Luke 22:7–13), we should note the related verb used in the account of Jesus' visit to Zacchaeus in Jericho: Jesus went "to be the guest [*katalusai*]" (Luke 19:7) of a notorious sinner, a chief tax collector (Luke 19:1–10; see Bovon, vol. 2, 590–602).

The identity (as "Lord" and "the Son of Man") and mission of Jesus ("to seek out and save the lost") are prominent in this meeting between Zacchaeus and Jesus. Zacchaeus begins by "wanting to see" the traveler and ends by recognizing him at a meal as "Lord" and showing his repentance by what he does and promises to do. As with the Passover to come, Jesus initiates this meal: "Zacchaeus, hurry and come down, for I must stay at your home today" (Luke 19:5). But then a critical audience ("all who saw it") grumble (Luke 19:7) at Jesus for agreeing to accept hospitality from a very disreputable man—unlike those involved in preparing the Passover, the last meal Jesus will eat with his disciples.

Jesus prepared to eat the Passover by sending Peter and John to the owner of a house in Jerusalem. They were to ask him what Jesus "the Master" told them: "where is the guest room [*kataluma*] where I may eat the Passover with my disciples?" (Luke 22:11). The house owner at once showed Peter and John "a large room upstairs, already furnished"; there they prepared the Passover (Luke 22:12).[17] Jesus knew in advance who would offer hospitality to him and his apostles. To be sure, "the inhabitants of Jerusalem were prepared to make space available to the pilgrims" who wanted to celebrate the Passover. "They were even expected to perform this service free of charge" (Bovon, vol. 3, 143). Nevertheless, without hesitation the anonymous house owner did what Jesus asked through Peter and John. While Jesus was in command of the situation, the three of them collaborated to put his plan into action; Jesus and his apostles could all sit down to eat the Passover meal.

By being able to eat in the privacy of a guest room upstairs—a *kataluma* in that sense rather than in the sense of being a public shelter for a random group of travelers—celebrating the Passover provided Christ and his core group of followers with a "wonderful intimacy."[18] The Jewish feast served "as a framework for the Last Supper of Jesus. This will become the first example of a new Christian rite, which itself will look forward to the banquet of the kingdom" (Bovon, vol. 3, 143–44).

At the Last Supper (Luke 22:15–20), Jesus defined in advance the meaning of his imminent death and resurrection—by the words of institution over the broken bread ("this is my body which is given for you") and the wine ("this cup is the new covenant in my blood, which is shed for you"). The "for you" pointed to the group sharing the meal with Jesus as the immediate beneficiaries of his death and new covenant. But, since Jesus called for the future repetition of the ritual ("do this in memory of me"), he wanted to confer on an indefinite number of others the saving benefits of his life, death, and resurrection. He desired to establish also with them his continuing place and presence in the meal fellowship he had instituted with a small, core group of disciples.[19]

The Last Supper came at the end of a life that began in Bethlehem with a birth outside the shelter of a public *kataluma*, moved through a ministry that included the parable of the Good Samaritan, assisted by the Good Innkeeper, and ended with a final celebration in a Jerusalem *kataluma*. The command "do this in memory of me" (Luke 22:19) extended beyond the ritual established on the eve of Jesus' death to concern his whole story, and hence the three inns that punctuated it. Thus "doing this in memory of me" can *also* be understood as an invitation to show the hospitality that failed at the birth of Jesus but that was inculcated by the parable of the Good Samaritan and supremely exemplified by Jesus the Good Innkeeper in an upper room of Jerusalem.

Ignatius proposed for retreatants a contemplation of the nativity that included overtones of the cross and resurrection. Attention to the three inns of Luke's Gospel fills out further possibilities for that contemplation. Like Mary at the end of the visit of the shepherds, we can "treasure all these words/events (*rēmata*) and ponder them in our hearts" (Luke 2:19).

THE LIFE AND MINISTRY OF CHRIST

After contemplating on the third day of the Second Week how the boy Jesus returns with his parents to Nazareth, the retreatants read a brief preamble for considering states of life (SpEx 135) and spend the fourth day meditating on what Ignatius calls the "two standards" and "three classes of persons" (SpEx 136–57). He dedicates the fifth day to contemplating Jesus' departure from Nazareth and his baptism in the Jordan (SpEx 158–60). Then follow seven days contemplating Jesus' life and ministry, through and including the events of Palm Sunday. Ignatius wants the exercitants to open their hearts to the teaching and example of Christ before making any choice of vocation or reform of life (SpEx 164). He knew that many of those making the Exercises were not yet in a situation to make an election after becoming free of disordered attachments.

This chapter will first sketch major lessons to be drawn from the Two Standards and the Three Classes. It will then suggest contemplating (2) the baptism of Jesus, and (3) what we read of Peter's mother-in-law's relationship to Jesus in Mark's Gospel. This path could be one way of entering into the life and ministry of Jesus and so being enabled to know him more clearly, love him more dearly, and follow him more nearly. All this serves to prepare retreatants to discern and decide what form, under the

Standard of Christ, decisions should take about their vocation in life or reform of life.

Ignatius's scheme proposes a contemplation of Andrew, Peter, and other male disciples accepting the call to follow Jesus (SpEx 161, 275), and it does so by outlining briefly the points for prayer. Here we offer longer reflections not only from contemporary biblical scholarship but also from some insights modern exegetes have missed. All this illuminates how Peter's mother-in-law met and reacted to Jesus.

THE TWO STANDARDS AND THREE CLASSES

The meditation on the Two Standards or Banners (SpEx 136–48) is the second bookend for those who prayerfully consider the incarnation/nativity of Jesus. The first bookend is a briefer, less imaginative call of the earthly king, a parable for gaining a first insight into the life of the Eternal King, Jesus Christ (SpEx 91–99). Through these two meditations a sense of sorrow and gratitude carries over from the First Week; this sense figures among the immediate prerequisites for a God-inspired discernment of and decisions about one's life-choice or deepening of a life-choice already made.

The meditation on the Two Standards pictures a struggle between (1) the spiritual forces of evil, with Lucifer, "the deadly enemy of our human nature" (SpEx 136), leading these enemy forces of deception, and (2) the spiritual forces of good that let us know "the true life revealed" by Christ, our commander-in-chief (SpEx 139).[1]

Ignatius emphasizes the way a universal campaign of satanic illusions infiltrates every human situation in the world and finally leads only to the unfreedom of self-centered pride. Lucifer sends demons to every place, state of life, and individual, aiming at enslaving all people with a false craving for riches. The more they have, the more they need. From this vice, they can be more readily led to lust after empty honors (being esteemed as a celebrity?) and, finally, indulging unbounded pride (SpEx

142). We could speak of the false self-security of achievements and possessions; the will to be honored and respected; and pride over what one has done and what, by way of consequence, one is supposed to be.

Christ, instead, sends his friends[2] and servants out to help everyone move at least toward a "spiritual poverty," that is to say, a "spiritual freedom" that does not allow itself to become enslaved to wealth. Thus they can avoid hungering after false honors and a completely self-centered pride, and so falling into other vices. They follow the teaching of Jesus about the value of "treasure in heaven" ("where your treasure is there is your heart also" [Matt 6:19–21]).

Thus the value system of Christ expounds, in this order: poverty as opposed to riches; insults or vulnerability as opposed to honors; and humility (or unselfish or agapeic love) as opposed to pride (SpEx 146, 147). Bearing insults and injustices may also involve coming to terms with past hurts through accepting the grace of forgiveness and healing.[3]

Some find it strange to put greed for material goods (and the false securities they can bring) in first place among the vices, with "spiritual poverty" correspondingly first among all the other virtues (SpEx142, 146). This insight emerged from what Ignatius experienced of Europe in the sixteenth century. Four centuries later, during the Second World War, David Gascoyne (1916–2001) wrote of "Christian warriors/Defending faith and property" in a world where "fear and greed are sovereign lords." His poem (*Ecce Homo*) anticipated prophetically the widespread recognition today that human greed has ravaged, perhaps beyond redemption, the planet with which we have been entrusted. We have been deceived into living a false way of life that fails to care for our common home, the earth. The widespread practice of a true "spiritual poverty" could well be the only solution to global destruction.

A now classic book by a modern German theologian, Johannes Baptist Metz (1928–2019), *Poverty of Spirit*,[4] describes what it means to be truly human. Either we accept poverty of spirit, or we lapse into unhealthy forms of living. "A person with grace," Metz writes, "is someone who has been emptied, who

stands impoverished before God, who has nothing to boast of....
It [poverty of spirit] is the doorway through which we must
pass to become authentic human beings. Only through poverty
of spirit do we draw near to God; only through it does God draw
near to us."[5]

Another radical conviction underpins the meditation on the
Two Standards: evil is ugly; Christ is the divine beauty and grace
in person (SpEx 140, 144). Lucifer, the supreme embodiment of
evil, is a "hideous and fearful figure" who sits upon a throne,
while the uniquely beautiful Christ stands with his friends. His
banner of beauty rises against the banner of ugly evil.[6] Once the
beauty of Christ has deeply touched us, no forces or illusions can
separate us from him (Rom 8:38–39).

Ignatius prescribes three repetitions of the Two Standards.
Such repeated meditations often pursue paths suggested by the
consolation and/or the desolation experienced in the original
meditation. In this case, one repetition might take up what I have
called the bookends to the incarnation and nativity: namely, (1)
the Call of the Earthly King and the Life of the Eternal King and
(2) The Two Standards. Comparing and contrasting closely the
two bookends could bring spiritual fruit by noting how the Two
Standards goes further. This meditation draws attention to the
enemy involved, the deceptions about a true life spread by the
forces of evil, and other items—not least the unique beauty of
Christ.

A triple colloquy (to the Virgin Mary, her Son, and the
Father) enhances the significance of the meditation on the Two
Standards (SpEx 147–48). This extended colloquy *does the same*
for the meditation on Three Classes of Persons that follows
immediately after three repetitions of the Two Standards (SpEx
149–157).[7]

Where the meditation on the Two Standards concerns *knowing* "the true life" and not merely imitating Christ "more closely"
(SpEx 139, 147), the meditation on the Three Classes aims at
choosing whatever serves better the glory of God and my personal
salvation (SpEx 152). This meditation acts as a reality check for
our human will. Am I truly free and at peace as I approach the
elections about the choice of vocation or the reform of my life?

The meditation on the Three Classes imagines people advanced in the spiritual life who experience an extraordinary, financial windfall. Ignatius talks about receiving ten thousand ducats, while we might think of a windfall profit on an investment. These groups ask themselves the question: "What is more for the glory of God and my salvation?"

Members of the first group allow this question to come up, recognize their attachment to the vast windfall, but do nothing to remedy the situation. They vaguely desire to be free from merely human attachments that will determine the outcome, but never take the means to do so.

The second group wishes to be free from their attachment to the money but wants to be spiritually free in such a way as to keep possession of the money. God can come into the picture, but only in the sense of approving what they have already decided.

The third group brings the issue to God, acting in the meantime as if they had already given up the money. They desire only to serve God better and do so in greater freedom than ever.

No meditation shows more vividly the psychological insights of Ignatius the spiritual director. In similar situations of decision, this meditation should be constantly deployed outside the Spiritual Exercises.

THE BAPTISM OF CHRIST

Ignatius dedicates the fifth day of the Second Week emphatically to the baptism of Jesus (SpEx 258–60, 273). He assigns to it a contemplation at midnight and in the morning, followed by two repetitions and, at the end of the day, an application of the senses.

On all occasions the retreatants should end with the triple colloquy, which Ignatius has already prescribed (SpEx 147, 156) and introduced in the setting of sin during the First Week (SpEx 62–63). At the start of the Second Week this colloquy was deployed to support the prayer made for the contemplations of the incarnation (SpEx 101) and the nativity (SpEx 110): to know interiorly the Lord who took on the human condition for me, so that I may love and follow him better (SpEx 104).

The story of Jesus' baptism (Matt 3:13–17) is an amazing scenario. Picture it: at the bottom you see Jesus coming out the waters of the river Jordan. Above him, the heavens are opened and the Holy Spirit descends on him in the form of a dove. Right at the top, a voice resounds out of heaven, saying, "This is my beloved Son with whom I am well pleased."

It is extraordinary drama: the voice of the Father ringing out above, the Spirit coming down under the appearance of the dove, and the beloved Son of God emerging from the river Jordan. The Gospel stories present a unique scene, revealing the tripersonal God. The heavens open, and God is disclosed to us as Father, Son, and Holy Spirit.

Matthew begins his story of Jesus' work on earth by putting before us this sensational tableau: the self-manifestation of God as three-in-one. What follows in the Gospel will develop and unfold this picture from the baptism of Jesus: the picture of God revealed as Father, Son, and Holy Spirit. The scene at the start of Matthew's Gospel sums up everything that will follow. *This is our God*, the God who is three-in-one, the God who has come among us and will be with us until "the end of the ages" (Matt 28:20).

But why is this revelation uniquely important? What difference would it make if God were simply one, not three-in-one, and not made known as Father, Son, and Holy Spirit? The astonishing heart of what was revealed at Jesus' baptism is this: God is a holy family. God is *the* Holy Family, the Three-in-One who live together in an ecstatic communion of love.

One of the most remarkable modern hymns to the Trinity is Brian Wren's "How Wonderful the Three-in-One," a hymn that sings of their "communing love in shared delight." These words apply beautifully to the ecstatic life that the Father, Son, and Holy Spirit have shared together from all eternity. They live *with* one another and *for* one another in an infinite ecstasy of love.

This Divine Family shows all of us what to do with our lives and how to let our lives become an existence of communing love. The Holy Family that is the Blessed Trinity forms the central role model for human life. We lose nothing but receive everything by sharing in that divine love, a divine love that wants everyone to be a winner and no one to be a loser.

PETER'S MOTHER-IN-LAW

The Gospel of Mark dedicates only three verses to the healing of Peter's mother-in-law (Mark 1:29–31). But these verses have much to say and imply—not least about her call to discipleship. Examining, comparing, and contrasting some commentaries on Mark can bring out the theological and spiritual richness to be found here. It may also reveal how sometimes experts pass over significant items.

Dennis Nineham

When commenting on the cure of Peter's mother-in-law from fever, Dennis Nineham opens by remarking that immediately prior to this cure, "the messianic power of Jesus" dealt with "a case of demonic possession. Now we learn that it can also deal with other forms of sickness."[8] To deliver from possession, "the power of Jesus worked through a word; here there is an action—*he took her by the hand and lifted her up*—but no word is reported."

Nineham points out the "impression of a cure performed effortlessly" and suggests that the reference to her serving "them" (Jesus, Peter, and three other disciples) presumably means "at table." Her immediate service illustrates "the completeness of the cure" and "its miraculous speed." Apropos of the last comment, Nineham cites St. Jerome: "the human constitution is such that after fever our bodies are rather tired, but when the Lord bestows health, restoration is immediate and complete."

Like other commentators, Nineham fails to say that Peter's mother-in-law is the first woman mentioned in Mark. Two of the other Gospels also report her cure (Matt 8:14–15; Luke 4:38–39), but by then they have recalled numerous women, notably Mary in their infancy narratives. It is the mother-in-law of Peter, not Tamar (Matt 1:3), Elisabeth (Luke 1:5), or anyone else who is the first woman to appear in Mark's Gospel.

Mark will refer later to other women: Jesus' mother Mary (3:31–35; 6:3); Jairus's daughter and the woman who touches Jesus' garment (5:21–43); a Syro-Phoenician woman (7:24–30); a widow who makes an offering in the temple (12:41–44); another woman left anonymous who anoints the feet of Jesus in the house of Simon the leper (14:3–9); and then numerous women, both named and unnamed, who attend Jesus' death and burial and are the first to learn of his resurrection (15:40–16:8)—not to mention Herodias and her daughter, who are directly responsible for the murder of John the Baptist (6:14–29), and the anonymous "servant-girl of the high priest" who identifies Peter as a follower of Jesus (14:66–69).[9] Yet the mother-in-law of Peter enjoys particular significance by being the first woman to appear in Mark's narrative.[10] While observing that the healing of Peter's mother-in-law "is the first account of the healing of a woman by Jesus in Mark," Susan Miller neglects to mention that she is the first woman *tout court* to be mentioned by Mark.[11]

Peter's mother-in-law stands out as the *only person* in Mark's Gospel who, after being cured by Jesus, does something for Jesus.[12] At table she serves him and others (specifically, her son-in-law and three other disciples), with her service mentioned as an appropriate response to being healed by Jesus. There may also be overtones of "victory over evil" being celebrated with messianic feasting. In Mark 2:18–20, Jesus will "describe his mission as a time of feasting."[13]

Nineham also remains silent about the significance and associations of the precise verb used of Peter's mother-in-law: "*diēkonei autois* [she began to serve them]." The same verb has already appeared when, in his brief account of Jesus' temptation, the evangelist ends by saying that "the angels served him" (Mark 1:12–13).[14] It will recur when Jesus declares that "the Son of Man has come not to be served but to serve, and to give his life as a ransom for many" (Mark 10:45). After Jesus has given his life on Calvary, we read of the presence at the crucifixion of Mary Magdalene and two other named women who "used to follow him and serve him when he was in Galilee; and there were many other women who had come up with him to Jerusalem"

(Mark 15:40–41). Nineham does not refer to the use of *serve* in these other contexts.[15]

Yet, as John Donahue and Daniel Harrington observe, "Peter's mother-in-law embodies and foreshadows the ideal of discipleship as service of others which Jesus will address to all the disciples." Through their ambitious request, James and John (Mark 10:35, 41), who were present at the healing of Peter's mother-in-law (Mark 1:29), prompt Jesus to insist that "the greatest among them should be their servant (*diakonos* [10:35–45, at 43])—an ideal Jesus himself incarnates (10:45)."[16]

Boring points out how *serve* resonates with "overtones of Christian ministry." The same verb will be used of Paul's "co-ministers, Timothy and Erastus" (Acts 19:22) and in Romans 15:25 of "Paul's own ministry." Thus "in ministering to Jesus and the disciples, this woman who has been healed and raised by Jesus performs a ministry analogous to later pastoral ministry."[17]

Before leaving Nineham, we should observe that he does not comment that the verb *egeirō* (raise up) will be used of the resurrection of people (12:26) and of Jesus (14:28; 16:6; see also, apropos of John the Baptist, 6:14, 16). The same verb will appear in the healing of a paralytic (2:9, 11) and of a man with a withered hand (3:3); in the resuscitation of Jairus's daughter (5:41); in the cure of an epileptic boy who had "become like a corpse" and seemed dead (9:26–27); and in the healing of blind Bartimaeus (10:49). Nineham does mention that, in speaking of Jesus' "raising up" Peter's mother-in-law, the Gospel introduces "a conventional Talmudic expression meaning to 'cure' or 'heal.'" Hence the action of Jesus can make us think of "various healings by rabbis in the Talmudic literature."[18] But this historical, extratextual comment neglects the subsequent and richly suggestive usage of *egeirō* within the narrative of Mark's Gospel itself.

Camille Foçant

In *The Gospel According to Mark: A Commentary*, Camille Foçant does, however, notice the rich cargo of meaning carried by the verbs *serve* and *raise up*. "At the first level, the service of Peter's mother-in-law agrees quite simply with the rules of hospitality."

But her service not only recalls the angels serving Jesus in the wilderness but also anticipates "a rare but important theme" that turns up later in Mark.[19] Foçant refers to the service of female disciples in Galilee (Mark 15:41) and leaves it at that.

After citing all the verses in Mark that feature *raise up* (listed above), Foçant describes the action of Jesus in raising up Peter's mother-in-law as "a symbolic theme whose harmonies will be developed in what follows." He does not press on to describe these "harmonies" that are to be developed. He does, however, dwell on a significant word order when, in the original Greek, Mark says that Jesus "raised her up, seizing her by the hand (*ēgeiren* [main verb] *autēn kratēsas* [aorist participle] *tēs cheiros*)." Nineham has played down this significance by reversing the order of the two verbs in the Greek text. He produces a translation that respects the normal chronological order we might expect: "he took her by the hand and lifted her up."[20] Foçant notes how, "in adopting the reverse presentation, Mark emphasizes the verb *egeirō*."[21] That lends, subsequently, more emphasis to the ways in which the evangelist will go on to use *raise up*. We return below to that subsequent usage.

Francis Moloney

Francis J. Moloney does not seem alert to this "reverse presentation" when he observes that "the miracle unfolds as a classical healing narrative: problem, request,[22] touch, miracle, demonstration."[23] In the text itself the sequence is rather: problem, (implicit) request, miracle, touch, and demonstration. But the heading Moloney provides for Mark 1:29–31 ("Jesus vanquishes sickness and taboo") shows that he is interested rather in Jesus seeming to break taboos by touching a woman and letting her serve him, as well as violating the Sabbath by performing a healing. He "could well be accused of contracting uncleanness and violating the Sabbath."[24]

But breaking such taboos seems more to the fore when Jesus touches a leper (Mark 1:41) and when a woman with permanent hemorrhages touches Jesus' clothing (Mark 5:25–34). The healing of Peter's mother-in-law takes place not in the public setting of these two miracles but in the home of two friends, Peter and Andrew, to which Jesus will return (Mark 2:1). As for violating the Sabbath, that issue moves center stage later: in the healing of a disabled person on the Sabbath and in a very public place, a synagogue (Mark 3:1–6). Apropos of Jesus taking the hand of Peter's mother-in-law, Moloney's doctoral supervisor, Morna Hooker, far from thinking of a taboo being broken, remarks that "as so often in healings of this kind in Mark, he [Jesus] heals through physical contact with the patient." Jesus touches "patients" (Mark 1:41; 5:41; 6:5; 7:32–33; 8:22–25), or is touched by them (Mark 3:10; 5:27–31; 6:56). Hooker thus connects the healing of Peter's mother-in-law with other such miracles in Mark's Gospel and introduces it with the title "Jesus Heals a Friend."[25]

Some may consider it slightly optimistic to call Peter's mother-in-law "a friend," at least at this point in the narrative. But certainly she is related to disciples who are already Jesus' close friends, Simon Peter and his brother Andrew. Hooker's choice of title implicitly recalls that, in Mark's Gospel, Peter's mother-in-law is the only person healed by Jesus with whom he already has or will come to have a personal relationship. All the others cured by him are strangers, who are brought to him (such as the paralytic in Mark 2:1–12), who have sought him out (such as the woman in Mark 5:24–34), who find themselves in his presence (the epileptic boy in Mark 9:14–29, for example), or whose cure is requested by someone who went looking for Jesus (the daughter of the Syro-Phoenician woman in Mark 7:24–30). The only, partial exception is Bartimaeus, who, after being cured, becomes a follower of Jesus "on the way" (Mark 10:46–52). Prior to being healed, Bartimaeus does not enjoy a personal relationship with Jesus. He has heard about Jesus, but that is all.

Judgments vary. But it seems to me that the healing of Peter's mother-in-law enjoys richer and clearer significance in ways not mentioned by Moloney (or Hooker). The first woman to be mentioned in Mark's Gospel and the only person healed by Jesus who then "serves" him, she helps produce an *inclusio*, as we shall see, with Mark 15:40—16:8.[26] The story of her healing uses the language of "raising up" and "serving," which play important roles in Mark's narrative. Moloney says nothing about the verb *egeirō*, which makes its first appearance in Mark's narrative through the healing of Peter's mother-in-law, and refers only briefly in a footnote to a "discipleship of service."[27]

Joel Marcus

When expounding "the symbolic significance for Mark's readers," Joel Marcus appreciates the relevance of the phrase in Greek "about Jesus grasping the woman's hand" coming "*after* 'he raised her.'" "This unusual position may be designed to concentrate attention" not on a taboo being broken (Moloney), but "on the charismatic power of Jesus' touch, which Mark elsewhere emphasizes" (see also Hooker[28]). But Marcus considers "even more significant the verb used to describe Jesus lifting the woman from her sickbed *ēgeiren* ('he raised'); the same verb is used in the story of the resuscitation of a dead girl in 5:41–42." This verb, Marcus believes, "would probably also have reminded Mark's readers of the general resurrection of the dead (12:26) and of Jesus' resurrection in particular." Thus Mark "probably wishes to imply" that the "raising power" revealed "in Jesus' healing miracles was the same eschatological power by which God later resurrected him from death."[29] Thus Marcus spells out what Focant merely refers to as "a symbolic theme whose harmonies will be developed in what follows."

Marcus also goes beyond Focant by commenting that the verb employed to report the service at table offered by the healed woman "was used to describe the angels' support of Jesus during his testing by Satan" (Mark 1:13). The "ministry of Peter's mother-in-law" "literarily mirrors that of the angels and anticipates that of Jesus himself (Mark 10:45)."[30] Marcus might have added that her "serving" Jesus also anticipates what three named women and "many [other] women" do in Galilee before they go up to Jerusalem and witness the crucifixion (Mark 15:40–41).

Presenting Mark's place "in Christian life and thought," Marcus includes a discussion of links between Mark and Paul.[31] Tentatively one might add to those links a certain prefiguration between the experience of Peter's mother-in-law and the experience of Christian baptism. After being raised from a life-threatening sickness, she at once dedicates herself to serving Christ and others. Paul describes baptism as sharing in Christ's death and resurrection, so that we might "walk in newness of life" (Rom 6:3–4; see 6:1–23).[32] The brief account of the healing of Peter's mother-in-law as "being raised" and then "serving" seems analogous to the vision of baptism presented by Paul. With the baptized she shares a death/life experience and then, through her service, behaves like a baptized person who is committed to a discipleship of service.

Sensitive to hints of "women's domestic servitude,"[33] Deborah Krause challenges those—including such feminists as Luise Schottroff, Elisabeth Schüssler Fiorenza, and Mary Ann Tolbert— who understand Peter's mother-in-law to be an example of early Christian discipleship. I believe the majority to be correct here. Without entering the full debate, I find Krause's argument less than convincing. Let me mention one detail; she states that "the references to *diakoneō* in Mark 1:31 and 15:41 are different."[34] Of course, they are *partly* different in their contexts: the verb refers in the first context to what an individual did at a specific family meal in Galilee and in the second context to what a large group, now present at a crucifixion, had been doing (also in Galilee) over a period of time prior to this tragic execution. But it would be quite gratuitous to allege that "these and other references" to this verb—it would be preferable to speak of usages of this verb— are different in meaning. Schüssler Fiorenza and others are correct in holding some consistency and overlap in the usage and meaning of *diakonein* in Mark.[35]

Summing Up

This sampling of comments by eight biblical scholars on the story of the healing of Peter's mother-in-law pays respect, I hope, to their valuable observations, as well as introducing some additions and corrections that appear necessary.

What seems a little surprising is, firstly, that none of the eight exegetes alerts readers to the fact that, in Mark's Gospel, Peter's mother-in-law is the first woman to appear and the only person who is cured by Jesus and then does something for him.[36]

One might have expected Adela Yarbro Collins to have noted these two points, but she fails to do so. All she does is refer to Krause's chapter as "a nuanced feminist reading" of the cure of Peter's mother-in-law.[37] Secondly, the language of "raising" and "serving" used in the account of the mother-in-law's healing and then, in a reverse order, of "serving" and "raising" at the close of this Gospel (15:41 and 16:6) encourages us—along with other data—to recognize a certain *inclusio* between the opening and ending of Mark.[38] At the outset in Galilee, a woman who is Peter's mother-in-law and lives in his house is "raised" and then begins to "serve" Jesus and four of his male disciples. At the end, her action is recalled by the women who, after following and "serving" Jesus in Galilee, then came to Jerusalem and were present at his crucifixion; three of them were the first to know of his being raised. Peter's mother-in-law may even have been one of those women courageously there on Calvary (among the "many other women" of Mark 15:41). Peter failed to turn up at Calvary. It would be supremely ironic if his mother-in-law were there.

Many commentators rightly recognize how Peter, the leading disciple, whom Jesus calls in Galilee (Mark 1:18–19), features in an *inclusio*. Richard Bauckham has recognized that and gone further by presenting, albeit not exclusively, "the Petrine perspective" of the entire Gospel of Mark. Peter's call is quickly followed by the healing of his mother-in-law in the very house in Galilee where he lives and over which she presides. The main eyewitness in Mark's Gospel, he is then the last disciple to be named and, in fact, named in connection with Galilee (Mark 16:7).[39]

But along with an *inclusio* in which Peter is central, we can also recognize an enlarged *inclusio* in which his mother-in-law also figures. This accentuates rather than reduces the rich significance of the healing narrative in which we meet her (Mark 1:29–31). The enlarged *inclusio* (between Mark 1 and 15/16) includes Jesus, Peter, an act of "raising" from a deadly situation, an anonymous mother-in-law/other anonymous women, the context of Galilee, and the service of Jesus (and others).

What, then, should be added to all that we might glean from existing commentaries on Mark's account of the healing of Peter's mother-in-law? First, her significance is announced by the fact that she is the *first woman* mentioned by Mark, who identifies her not by name but through her relationship to the leading disciple, her son-in-law Simon Peter. Second, she stands out as the *only person* in that Gospel (with the possible exception of Bartimaeus) who is cured by Jesus and then does something for him. The anonymous woman in Mark 14:3–9 performs a very significant action for Jesus, by anointing him in advance of his burial. But she does this without his having healed her.[40] Third, the language of "raising" and "serving" used in the account of the cure of Peter's mother-in-law, along with its location (in the Galilean house of Peter and Andrew, who have just been called to become disciples), locates her in the initial material that will be taken up again in Mark's closing verses. Any *inclusio* involving Peter brings in, rather than excludes, his mother-in-law.

The next chapter continues with further material for contemplation taken from the Gospels and does so with the freedom of choice that Ignatius allows for (SpEx 162). We will look at the call of Matthew and then turn to the transfiguration and two miracles from John's Gospel. The chapter will end with considerations taken from Ignatius's directives about one's choice of vocation or reform of one's life in following a vocation already chosen.

8

MORE FROM JESUS' LIFE, AND THE ELECTIONS

In presenting the first two contemplations, the Call of Matthew and the Transfiguration, I will use a brief essay form. For the third and fourth contemplations, Jesus' healing in John's Gospel of a man disabled for thirty-eight years and then of a man blind from birth, I will follow Ignatius's system of points but supply more than his customary three. For the preparatory prayer and the preambles, this chapter presupposes the method that Ignatius has outlined at the start of the Second Week (SpEx 101–5). It ends with the "elections" and the reform of life.

THE CALL OF MATTHEW

"Jesus saw a man called Matthew, sitting at a tax booth, and he said to him, 'Follow me'" (Matt 9:9). Once again tourists are visiting the church of St. Louis in Rome to see three masterpieces painted by Caravaggio. You find the three paintings on the left, in a chapel dedicated to St. Matthew. The first painting depicts Matthew sitting at his tax booth engaged in the unsavory work of collecting taxes, but now called by Christ to leave that disreputable occupation and become a disciple. The second painting represents Matthew writing his Gospel. The third painting portrays the martyrdom of Matthew.

Whenever I went into that church, I found a steady stream of visitors. They were headed for the chapel of St. Matthew and gazed in awed silence at those works by Caravaggio. After absorbing the genius of the three masterpieces, most people went away with a sense of which was their favorite painting.

My own choice is the first painting, which portrays Matthew being called to become a disciple of Jesus. On the one side, Christ stretches out his arm and evokes Michelangelo's depiction of the creation of Adam in the Sistine Chapel. On the other side, there is Matthew sitting at his desk with light shining on his face. He has seen and recognized the divine Light that has come into the world. Behind the outstretched arm of Christ there is an open window; its woodwork takes the form of a cross.

In brilliant fashion, Caravaggio associates the creation of the world, our creation, with the incarnation and the divine Light that has come into the world. He also links creation with the call of Matthew to follow Christ, who will be crucified on the wood of the cross. Thus, Caravaggio brings together creation, the incarnation, and the crucifixion.

Matthew himself was blessed in three marvellous ways. He was brought into existence by God. He saw and accepted the divine Light that shone on the face of Christ. He was called to share in a mission to the world which involved the crucifixion of Christ and his own that imitated the passion of his Master.

Caravaggio's painting of Matthew's call brings together three basic and enormous blessings that have shaped our lives. We have been created and brought into existence. We have seen the glory of God on the face of Christ. We are called as baptized believers to take our part in a mission to the whole world, which involves the passion of Christ and our own share in that passion.

Matthew showed immediately his joy and gratitude at the ways he had been blessed. He invited Jesus to his home, put on a big dinner, and began at once his own mission by drawing other morally disreputable persons into the saving presence of Jesus (Matt 9:9–13). We must show our joy and gratitude at the ways we too have been richly blessed through the healing and redeeming presence of Christ our Lord.

THE TRANSFIGURATION OF JESUS

When Luke tells the story of the transfiguration (9:28–36), he specifies that Jesus "went up on the mountain to pray." It was "while he was praying" that his face changed, his clothing shone brilliantly, and Moses and Elijah appeared "in glory" and spoke with him about his "departure" or coming death, resurrection, and ascension.

Peter, James, and John had climbed the mountain with Jesus for some quiet prayer and now found themselves sharing an intense religious experience. Right there in their presence, Jesus was transfigured, and he had been joined by two persons who went the distance for God: Moses, the liberator and lawgiver, and Elijah, the great prophet. The three disciples "saw the glory" of Jesus and of the two heavenly visitors who stood talking with him.

The Bible has much to say about the "glory" or radiant splendor of God, something that is very close to the divine beauty. When the Psalmist declares, "The heavens show forth the glory of God," that amounts to saying, "The heavens show forth the beauty of God" (Ps 19:1). After the destruction of the city, Isaiah promises that, when Jerusalem is restored, the luminous beauty of God will appear over it (Isa 60:1–5). Not only in the heavens above but also in the holy city here on earth the beauty of God can be seen.

Peter, James, and John saw in advance something of the glorious beauty that would shine forth from Christ when he was risen from the dead. Their hearts were on fire. Hardly knowing what he was saying, Peter volunteered to preserve and prolong this enthralling vision of beauty by making three dwellings: one for Jesus, one for Moses, and one for Elijah.

Peter reacted the way we all do when carried away by some enchanting experience. Years ago at the Salzburg Festival, the young Claudio Abbado set on fire the hearts of a huge audience by the brilliant way he conducted Beethoven's Seventh Symphony. Along with thousands of others who had come from around the world, I did not want that experience of beauty to end. We can all remember such intense experiences that made us incredibly happy, experiences that we wanted to last forever.

But more was to come for Peter, James, and John. A cloud swept over them and terrified them. From the shining cloud came the voice of God: "This is my chosen Son; listen to him."

Before the three disciples had time to inwardly digest their awesome experience, it suddenly ended. Moses and Elijah disappeared; the cloud was gone; the divine voice fell silent; the radiant beauty slipped away from the face and body of Jesus. Quite abruptly Peter, James, and John found themselves alone with their Master on the mountain.

Overwhelmed by their awe-inspiring and fascinating experience, the three disciples kept it to themselves for some time. They had been uniquely privileged: they had seen the coming beauty of Christ unveiled before their eyes; and they had heard the very voice of God.

When they came down, they took to heart the vision of Christ's divine beauty they had been granted on the mountain. From now on they could focus their attention only on the glorious Son of God and give him their lifelong obedience.

Every now and then in our lives, we may be tempted to feel like that character in a novel by Saul Bellow. He found life to be a nightmare during which he was trying to get some sleep. Or, to quote a question from the Roman philosopher Seneca: "Why weep for the end of life? The whole of it deserves our tears."

But Jesus deals with our tears and nightmares. We enjoy the sure knowledge of his triumph over death on the cross, the "departure" of which Moses and Elijah spoke. It became Jesus' passage to a glory that will never end.

The last book of the Bible, the Book of Revelation, fills out the glimpse of glory conveyed by Jesus' transfiguration. God will make a home among human beings and will "wipe every tear from their eyes. Death will be no more; mourning and crying and pain will be no more." These things will have passed away. A cosmic transformation will bring "the new heaven and the new earth" (Rev 21:1–4).

The transfiguration of Jesus led to his glorious, heavenly transformation. What he experienced on the mountain promised that such a transformation would be his destiny and the destiny of those who follow him. The God who spoke to the three disciples on the mount of transfiguration is utterly faithful to all who lean on him as their "light and salvation."

During the journey of our retreat, let us go up the mountain to pray with Jesus. May we, too, see something of his divine beauty that will set our hearts on fire. If we do, we will be enabled to focus our attention on him and give him our lifelong allegiance.

A briefer scheme for contemplating the transfiguration based on Mark 9:2–8 can be set out in five points: (1) Moses and Elijah join Jesus in the glory of the transfiguration. He will die in the company of two unnamed persons. (2) The clothes of Jesus become dazzlingly white. On Calvary he will be stripped of his garments. (3) The voice of the Father affirms the identity of Jesus. On Calvary a Roman centurion will confess the identity of Jesus. (4) At the transfiguration, Peter, James, and John are "terrified" (Mark 9:6). On Calvary the Roman centurion is awed at the divine manifestation in Christ's death (Mark 15:39). (5) Three male followers of Jesus witness the transfiguration. On Calvary three named women disciples, along with a group of anonymous women. witness the crucifixion.

The mysteries of Christ's life listed by Ignatius (SpEx 261–312) do not include any parables. Many directors of the Exercises have judged it suitable to introduce the parable of the prodigal son (Luke 15:11–32). Likewise, apart from the raising of Lazarus from the dead (John 11:1–45; SpEx 161, 285), no healing miracles make the Ignatian list. Two healing stories in John's Gospel recommend themselves for contemplation. I set them out schematically, but do not follow the terseness of Ignatius.

THE MAN DISABLED FOR THIRTY-EIGHT YEARS AND THE MAN BORN BLIND

- The man disabled for thirty-eight years (John 5:1–18) fell into that condition before Jesus was born. He had given up on himself, having become utterly used to the crippled situation in which he found himself.

- He cannot go looking for Jesus, as Nicodemus (chapter 3) or the official from Capernaum (chapter 4) do. Jesus picks him out as the one who seems most in need.
- Jesus tries to rouse a little hope: "Do you want to be healed?" The man excuses himself for not having been cured when the waters were stirred up and enjoyed healing powers: "Sir, I have no one to put me into the pool when the water is stirred up."
- The man's situation is tragic; he lives so close to a pool that every now and then possesses powers of healing. He cannot take the small step that would save him.
- Jesus heals him. The man who could not even move himself now carries away his bed. But he is not fully healed; he does not "know" Jesus.
- Jesus seeks him out: "See, you are well; sin no more, so that nothing worse befall you." But the man anticipates Judas, betraying Jesus' name to those who are outraged at a healing on the sabbath.

We turn now to the man blind from birth (John 9:1–41).

- The disciples are blind to the man's suffering and Jesus' power. They treat the man as the subject for a theological discussion: "Rabbi, who sinned, this man or his parents?"
- The man does not say anything but is presumably heartened by what he hears Jesus say. Then Jesus takes the initiative and anoints the man's eyes. Now the blind man has something to do; he must go and wash his eyes in the pool of Siloam.
- Jesus leaves the stage (John 9:7b–34). The man begins to act vigorously and suffer. He is brought into conflict with his parents and the religious authorities.
- The man moves from truth to truth about Jesus: "prophet," "from God," and the "Lord" in whom

he believes. He trusts and discerns his experience: "one thing I know, that though I was blind, now I see." "Never since the world began has it been heard that anyone opened the eyes of a man born blind."

- While the man born blind is physically blind, the disciples and some Pharisees are spiritually blind. The chapter is dominated by words for blindness, eyes, and sight: the expression "to open the eyes" is used seven times. Our eyes need to be opened by Jesus, who is the Light of the world.

ELECTIONS AND REFORM OF LIFE

As a prelude to the elections, Ignatius recommends that retreatants spend an entire day turning over in their mind and heart what he calls "Three Kinds of Humility," or what some have renamed as "Three Kinds of Unselfish Love" (SpEx 165–68). The first kind means subjecting ourselves to the basic divine and human laws that bind us seriously—that is to say, laws that are necessary for our eternal salvation. We keep these laws, even (or especially?), as has been said, when no one is looking. As Ignatius puts it, the first kind will not deliberately agree to commit mortal sins.

The second kind goes further and will not deliberately agree to commit venial sin. This kind of humility invites the retreatants to practice what the Principle and Foundation has called an "indifference," which does not prefer, seek, or desire *wealth* rather than poverty, *fame,* or celebrity status rather than disgrace, and a *long life* rather than a short life. Disordered interests that desire at all costs wealth, fame, and good health can predetermine life-decisions.

The third kind presupposes the first two kinds of unselfish love but goes beyond them by taking its shape from the *imitation of Christ* and choosing with him to be a poor nobody. Those who embrace it desire to be more like the poor and homeless Christ (see 2 Cor 8:9), whose crucifixion led him to be considered an idiotic failure by the wise and prudent of this world (see 1 Cor 1:18–23). They follow him in being vulnerable and homeless (Matt 8:20). Those who aspire to this third kind should employ the triple colloquy and ask for the grace to imitate and serve Christ better.

Opportunities to practice this third kind of humility have not disappeared in modern times; they have only relocated. Take, for example, the warning coming from the Second Vatican Council and directed to those who set themselves to promote justice and peace: "we must carry the cross which the flesh and the world inflict on the shoulders of those who seek after peace and justice" (*Gaudium et Spes*, The Church in the Modern World, 38, my translation).[1]

The preamble to making elections draws a warning from the Principle and Foundation. The *end* for which human beings have been created is to serve and praise God our Lord and so receive personal salvation. Retreatants must be convinced of the priority of this end over any means toward arriving at it. Refashioning the means so that they become the end of human existence is the equivalent of wanting God to come to us rather than our going to God (SpEx 169).

Distinguishing elections that involve changeable choices (such as the disposal of some material possessions) from those that involve, or should involve, unchangeable choices (marriage or priestly ordination, for example) (SpEx 170–74), Ignatius sets out three *times* and two ways for making a sound and good election (SpEx 175–88).

Ignatius cites St. Matthew (alongside St. Paul) as someone who exemplified the first time when he followed his call (see last chapter). God dramatically moved and attracted Matthew's will, so that he simply could not doubt that his choice was sound and good. Ignatius names as "dedicated souls" (SpEx 175) those who make a choice in this "first time." Although many who do so could deserve this designation, prior to his apostolic call, Matthew could hardly be named this way, whatever we make of Paul before his call.

In the second time the "*experience* of consolations and desolations," along with the "*experience* of the discernment of different spirits," will take some time and does not occur in a dramatic moment. But such experience can confirm a decision that supports the goal of my human existence, the service and praise of God that will bring the "salvation of my soul."

The third time embodies two ways for making a good and sound election. At the heart of the *first way* comes a reasoned calculus of all the advantages and disadvantages of a given choice—that is to say, advantages and disadvantages vis-à-vis the goal of human existence, the praise and service of God and our personal salvation. Retreatants should accept the conclusion that *reason* indicates, provided we sense that God "accepts and confirms" it. The decision should not leave us feeling uneasy, even though it may be supported only by 52 percent to 48 percent in calculating the advantages and disadvantages.

The *second way*, which is inspired by love, asks retreatants to imagine someone whom they have never met or known but who faces the same choice as they do. Desiring nothing but the best for such a person, what advice would they offer in order that the person give greater glory to God and further his or her own final salvation?

Ignatius follows up this very "objective" mode of proceeding with a very "subjective" method. The retreatants should think ahead to their death and put to themselves the question: On my death bed what decision would I then wish to have reached and followed here and now?

Ignatius completes the section on "elections" by adding a long paragraph to guide those whose situation allows only for the *reform* of their personal life and state and not for its radical change (SpEx 189). Such retreatants are urged to let their decisions be guided by nothing else than a desire to praise and glorify God in all things as well as to "save their souls."

Ignatius concludes this paragraph (and the Second Week) by remarking that "everyone must bear in mind that one will make progress in spiritual things to the extent in which one shall have put off self-love, self-will and self-interest." On the one hand, readers might bridle at the idea of "putting off" true self-love and recall the scriptural command to "love one's neighbor as oneself." There is, after all, a proper self-care and self-love.

Moreover, serving and praising God with all our heart will turn out for our true self-interest. On the other hand, a deadly selfishness falsely puts ourselves at the center of the universe.

Anthony de Mello engaged brilliantly with some of these issues in "unselfing the self," a section in *Seek God Everywhere: Reflections on the Spiritual Exercises of St. Ignatius,* and coming at the start of the Third Week.[2] To that week we now turn.

THIRD WEEK

THE PASSION AND DEATH
OF CHRIST

With the main purpose of the Spiritual Exercises achieved through choosing a state of life or reforming one's existing state of life, the Third Week and the Fourth Week serve to confirm the decisions already taken.

Right at the start, Ignatius employs, albeit in passing, the language of the "purgative" and "illuminative" ways (SpEx 10). During the second half of the sixteenth century various directories or commentaries on the Spiritual Exercises appeared. The 1599 *Directory* put the Third and Fourth Weeks together as the "unitive" way in a triple scheme of Christian perfection (purgative, illuminative, and unitive ways) that had become standard.[1] Ignatius's version of the unitive way was heavily colored by a compassion that desired to suffer "grief with Christ in grief" and "to be broken with Christ who is broken" (SpEx 203).

This chapter will examine the Third's Week primary focus, the place of the Blessed Virgin Mary in the presentation of the passion, a question for Ignatius about Christ's divine nature being "in hiding," and what the four Gospels offer retreatants.

PRIMARY FOCUS OF THE THIRD WEEK

The First and Second Weeks do not avoid invoking the cross. The First Week involves a striking colloquy with Christ hanging on the cross (SpEx 53). The contemplation on the nativity in the Second Week presents Christ "born in extreme poverty," so that "after so many labors, after hunger, thirst, heat and cold, outrages and affronts, he dies on the cross, and all this for me" (SpEx 110). The cross turns up implicitly through the theme of following Christ "in suffering," which we find in the Call of the King, the Two Standards, and the third Mode of Humility.

The Third Week focuses primarily on the crucifixion and seeks the grace of compassion, understood as "grief, deep feeling and confusion because it is for my sins that the Lord" is suffering the passion (SpEx 193). The 1599 Directory introduces four questions to open the suffering of Christ for contemplation: "Who is suffering? What is he suffering? At whose hands? For whom?" An intensely personal identification with Christ in his suffering gains a sense of immediacy through the repeated use of the present tense about the way he suffers (SpEx 193, 195–97). He does this for me and my sins (SpEx 193, 197).

THE LONELINESS OF OUR LADY

After proposing for prayer the taking down from the cross and burial of Jesus, Ignatius introduces the suffering of Mary in her "loneliness," "grief," and "exhaustion" (SpEx 208). Ignatius developed the Spiritual Exercises after the *Stabat Mater* (attributed to Jacopone da Todi, who died in 1306) had entered liturgical usage in the late Middle Ages. "The Mother standing [at the cross]" had also appeared in many masterpieces, down to the painting by Grünewald on the Isenheimer altar (completed before 1516). The *Pietà*, a statue or painting that represents Mary holding her dead Son after he had been taken down from the cross, developed from German origins in the thirteenth century and so long before Ignatius. Nevertheless, he declined to appeal to the grief of Mary either as she stood by the cross or received the dead body of Jesus. Apart from the triple colloquy (SpEx 199), Ignatius postponed any reference to Mary until Holy Saturday and her loneliness on that longest day in Christian history. This allowed, prayerfully and psychologically, a more dramatic preparation for the risen Jesus' appearance to his Mother (SpEx 219, 299).

Despite Ignatius's delay in introducing Mary, retreatants may make use of images of Mary at the foot of the cross. That scene invites them to imagine how the Mother of Jesus experienced the terrible suffering and humiliation of his crucifixion. They might also reflect on the body of Jesus held in the arms of Mary. The whole story of Jesus is preserved in his lifeless body. It allows the passion and death of Jesus to come home to them when they contemplate a version of the *Pietà*.

The earthly history of Jesus is written in his dead body. This "body language" allows us to look back and recall what he did for human beings during his lifetime and what they did for him. We might focus in turn on his eyes, his mouth, his ears, his hands, and his feet. I have set out at length the shape of such a fivefold contemplation.[2] Here, to exemplify what Ignatius would call "the points" for this prayer, let me take his *eyes*.

His eyes are closed: those eyes looked across crowds of men and women who were like sheep lost and anxious to find a true shepherd. His eyes smiled at children and blazed with anger at the religious leaders who put their version of the law above the needs of suffering people. His eyes filled with tears at the death of a beloved friend, gazed with compassion at the sick, and looked steadily at the disciples when he asked, "Who do you say that I am?"

At the end, what did Jesus see in his passion? Judas coming to betray him with a kiss, the other disciples fleeing through the olive trees in Gethsemane, and Peter breaking down in grief at having denied his Master. What did the eyes of Jesus see when he made his way to Calvary and then hung for several hours on the cross? And then those eyes finally closed, not in sleep but in death.

THE DIVINE NATURE GOING INTO HIDING

Ignatius famously wrote of "the divine nature going into hiding" during the passion. Being also divine by nature, Christ our Lord could have destroyed the enemies bent on putting him to death (Matt 26:53). But he allowed himself to suffer horribly "in his sacred human nature," and did so, not least to deliver me from my sins (SpEx 196–97).

Yet we need to modify the notion of Christ's divine identity being hidden in his suffering and death. According to Mark 15:39, the centurion in charge of Jesus' execution, seeing the way Jesus breathed his last, cried out, "Truly this man was the Son of God" (Mark 15:39). Right in the weakness and humiliation of his crucifixion, the divine identity of Jesus was unveiled.

John's Gospel pictures Jesus as completely in charge of the situation after a detachment of soldiers and temple police arrive to arrest him. They fall to the ground when confronted by Jesus, who, by revealing himself as "I am" (John 18:5–8), associates himself with God's self-revelation to Moses at the burning bush (Exod 3:14).

Great artists succeed in representing something of Jesus' divine identity being revealed even (or especially?) in his suffering. Rembrandt, for instance, showed a majestic and beautiful identity disclosed in the ugliness and weakness of Jesus' passion and death. The Dutch artist's images of Christ standing before Pilate, on the way to Calvary, and nailed to the cross let a powerful, beautiful identity gleam through the pain and weakness of suffering.

WHAT THE GOSPELS OFFER THE RETREATANTS

The four evangelists tell more or less the same passion story; yet significant differences emerge. These are, often brilliantly, expounded for preaching and prayer in Raymond E. Brown, *The Death of the Messiah*.[3] Steering close to the method of "points" adopted by Ignatius, let us take the Gospels in what seems to be the order of their composition.

In his passion story Mark repeatedly uses "hand over (*paradidōmi*)." Judas plans to "hand over" Jesus to his enemies (14:10–11, 21, 42, 44); the chief priests "hand Jesus over" to Pontius Pilate 15:1,10); Pilate "hands him over" (15:15) to be crucified.

No one stands by Jesus or speaks for him in the passion; his *loneliness* is striking.[4] Peter boasts, "We have left all things and followed you" (10:28). But when an armed crowd arrives to arrest Jesus, the disciples all flee—symbolized by the young man who flees naked into the night (14:50–52). They leave all things to get away from Jesus. Here Mark differs from Matthew (who recalls Pilate's wife telling her husband, "Have nothing to do with that innocent man" [Matt 27:19]) and Luke (who mentions the women who weep for Jesus and the "good thief" who turns to him in death [Luke 23:27, 39–43]). In Mark's passion story, it is only after Jesus' death and the tearing of the curtain of the temple (from top to bottom) that the centurion confesses, "Indeed, this man was the Son of God" (15:39) and that we learn of the presence of the many female disciples (15:40–41, 47) and of the act of Joseph of Arimathea in giving Jesus an honorable burial (15:42–47). Could retreatants put themselves into the story after 14:52 and imaginatively remedy the loneliness of Jesus during his passion?

Among the features of Matthew's story, retreatants might focus on the ways in which various people try to shake off their responsibility for the arrest and imminent death of Jesus (see chapter 4 above, n8). Judas wants to return the thirty pieces of silver to the chief priests and the elders. But they refuse to take back what he has been paid. So he flings the money down in the sanctuary and hangs himself (27:3–5). Even then the chief priests decline to put the money into the temple fund. They distance themselves from the money by using it to buy a place to bury foreigners (27:7–10). In the most famous gesture of human history, Pilate washes his hands in full view of the crowd (27:24). *The Passion*, a BBC documentary screened during Holy Week of 2008, seized on this gesture: Pilate alerted the audience in advance to what was to come on Good Friday by first washing his hands on Palm Sunday.

Who was responsible for the death of Jesus? Might we see Judas (a follower of Jesus), the chief priests (Jews), and Pilate (a Gentile) as representing all human beings and through their sins bringing about the death of Jesus? Matthew's passion story encourages us to answer yes to the question posed by the hymn, "Were you there when they crucified my Lord?"

Through the passion story of Luke, Jesus the Savior heals and forgives.[5] Retreatants might recall earlier passages in that Gospel that take up this theme: for example, "today is born for you a Savior" (2:11); "power came out of him and healed them all" (6:19). In the garden, Jesus makes a last-minute attempt to save Judas by acknowledging him by name ("Judas, would you betray the Son of man with a kiss?") (22:48). Jesus heals the right ear of the high priest's servant after Peter has cut it off with his sword (22:51). Likewise, in Luke Jesus "turns and looks at" Peter and prompts his "bitter" tears after denying his Master (22:61). It is only in Luke that Peter weeps "bitterly," and it is only then that Jesus gives him a forgiving and healing look.

Only Luke reports an episode that involved Herod Antipas and Pilate. Apparently there was a rift between Herod Antipas and Pilate. After Pilate sent Christ to Herod, this rift was healed and these "enemies" became "friends" (23:6–12). This unusual healing could foreshadow the reconciliation of God's people with the nations that Jesus brought about. On the way to Calvary Jesus shows deep concern for the women and their children (23:27–31). Similarly, it is only in Luke's passion story that Jesus prays for those putting him to death and promises final salvation to the good thief (23:34, 43). It is only in Luke that we hear of "all Jesus' acquaintances" being there at the crucifixion (23:49). Despite the failure of the male disciples, supremely exemplified by Peter's triple denial, somehow they are there and involved in the supreme healing event of the crucifixion.

Finally, we turn to John's passion story.[6] Let me focus only on John's version of Jesus' arrest (18:1–11). There he is, the Light of the world (1:4–9), the true source of warmth and vitality for all human beings. Judas leads a detachment of (Roman) soldiers and temple police, armed with "*lanterns, torches*, and weapons" to arrest the Light of the world. Ironically, these forces of darkness and death need some illumination; otherwise, they could not see the Light of the world. The irony surfaces a little later when Peter goes to the wrong source by warming himself at a charcoal fire (18:18). He relies on a charcoal fire instead of relying on the beautiful Light of the world.

In John's version of the arrest, Jesus is in complete command. "Knowing all that would come upon him," he does not wait to be identified and arrested but takes the initiative himself. He steps forward and asks the party of soldiers and police, "Who are you looking for?" Throughout John's Gospel, right from his first words ("what are you looking for" [1:38]), Jesus reveals himself as the One who questions those who are seeking him. These Jesus-seekers form two classes: those who seek him to receive life (Andrew and his companion in 1:38) and those who wish to do away with him. In the garden of Gethsemane it is those bent on killing him who are looking for him, and who will find him and arrest him.

When the soldiers and temple police state whom they are looking for, "Jesus of Nazareth," he replies, "I am (18:5)," a clear evocation of the divine name revealed to Moses at the burning bush (see Exod 3:14). Faced with the divine name and its numinous power, all those who had come to arrest Jesus, including Judas, step back and fall to the ground. The earthly power, which the Roman and temple authorities exercised through their soldiers and police, proves utterly feeble when confronted with the majestic authority of the incarnate Son of God.

When Jesus repeats what he has already said, he adds something that reaches to the heart of the passion narrative's meaning: "I told you that I am [Jesus of Nazareth]. So if you are looking for me, let these others go" (18:8). The others go free, but Jesus allows himself to be arrested and put to death for all others and for their everlasting benefit. He is the bread given and broken for the life of the world (6:51). Those others, entrusted to Jesus by his Father (18:9), are not merely the few persons with whom he has just shared a last meal, but all men and women of all times and places.

Such are some of the accents and insights we find in the passion stories of the four Gospels. For those making the Spiritual Exercises, a few points from one Gospel should provide sufficient material during the Third Week and support the principal objective, the confirmation of decisions already made about a change of life or a reform of life.

THE PASSION AND DEATH OF CHRIST

SOME RESOURCES FOR PRAYER

One way or another, Ignatius encourages prayerfully engaging with the whole passion story during the Third Week (SpEx 209). Perhaps nowadays we can best do this by contemplating the passion narrative of only one Gospel. Yet both within the Spiritual Exercises and beyond, retreatants can also draw spiritual "profit" from some liturgical and extra-liturgical practices, sacred music, art, and literature.

LITURGICAL AND OTHER PRACTICES

The legacy of Karl Rahner (1904–84) includes some liturgical homilies that reach the heart of the matter. His homily for Good Friday, published in *The Eternal Year*, highlights the practice of the *Veneration of the Cross* on which Christ died and the various classes of people who step forward to kiss, embrace, or kneel before the cross—from children, old people and the widowed, through to other groups, including priests themselves. They all lay down their burden of sin and suffering at the feet of the Crucified One. Rahner ends by echoing the procession of the cross: "I want to see the wood of the cross, on which the salvation of the world, my salvation, hung. Come let us adore him."[1]

The Stations of the Cross, popularized by the Franciscans in the later Middle Ages and so before the time of Ignatius, remain a widespread means for sharing through prayer in the passion, death, and burial of Jesus. St. Leonard of Port Maurice (1676–1751) erected more than five hundred sets of Stations in Europe, the most famous being the one in the Colosseum of Rome where popes have regularly led the faithful on Good Friday evening. Different spiritual graces emerge from the prayers repeated when making the Stations: for instance, "We adore you, O Christ, and we bless you, because by your holy cross you have redeemed the world."

Like the Stations of the Cross, the medieval passion plays elaborately presented the story of Jesus' suffering and death. These religious dramas have also enjoyed a striking revival since the nineteenth century—not least through the continuing success of the Oberammergau Passion Play (southern Bavaria), which has been staged more or less every ten years since 1634 and which over the last fifty years has shed some of its anti-Semitic elements. Other passion plays continue in Italy, Spain, and many other places in the world, including Trafalgar Square, London.

Presented by one hundred actors and volunteers of the Wintershall company and live streamed, *The Passion of Jesus* has two performances on Good Friday: at 12 noon and 3:15 pm. Each year around twenty thousand people pack into Trafalgar Square for this passion play.

Other practices conducive to assimilating the graces of the passion narratives clustered under the heading of devotion to the Sacred Heart, which developed in the Middle Ages through the Carthusians, the Franciscans, and others, such as St. Gertrude of Helfta, also known as Gertrude the Great (d. 1302). Oriented to the suffering of Christ and to the piercing of his side in death (John 19:31–37), this devotion highlighted the supreme place of the sacrificed and risen Christ's presence, the Eucharist.

The visions of St. Margaret Mary Alacoque (d.1690) encouraged making a Holy Hour before the Blessed Sacrament on Thursday night, united with Jesus' suffering and imaginatively praying in the Garden of Gethsemane. She saw the pierced heart of Jesus surrounded by a crown of thorns, surmounted by a cross and emitting flames of love. At times she saw the heart alone; at other times, Jesus appeared, showing his heart within his breast. The rays of love indicated divine triumph, but the heart, still wounded and bleeding and still pierced by thorns, recalled the suffering of his passion.

Ignatius alerts those who direct and those who make the Spiritual Exercises to the piercing of Christ's side and the blood and water that poured out (SpEx 297). Ignatius has already listed among the "mysteries" of Christ's life an episode found only in Luke's Gospel: "He sweated blood so abundantly" that "his sweat was like drops of blood that ran to the ground, which implies that his garments were full of blood" (SpEx 290).

These Lukan verses (22:43–44) have often been considered a later addition. They were, in any case, added from an ancient source and already cited by such second-century writers as Justin and Irenaeus.[2] Some scholars recognize these verses as coming from Luke himself: for instance, François Bovon. He comments, "The blood that clots outside his [Christ's] veins or arteries expresses the intensity of his fear physically. Jesus shares completely in the human condition."[3]

Devotions focused on the blood of Christ and his five wounds flourished in the Middle Ages. These devotions have been largely subsumed into devotion to the Sacred Heart. A mosaic by a contemporary Slovenian artist, Marko Rupnik, pictures the crucified Christ flanked by his Mother and a Roman soldier armed with long spear. The wounds and blood of Christ belong integrally to this work in which Mary's two hands direct the viewer to her Son's heart. I know the mosaic well, having requested it for the cover of my *The Beauty of Jesus Christ.*[4]

Ignatius also mentions what the tradition called "the seven words from the cross" and recalls them in detail—from the first (Jesus praying for those who crucified him) through to the seventh ("Father, into your hands I commend my spirit") (SpEx 297). Although we are dealing with utterances taken from the passion narratives of the four canonical Gospels and not with single words, traditionally they have been called "words" on/from the cross.

Ignatius inherited this devotion from the late Middle Ages. Later it was developed in Peru after a devastating earthquake of 1678 and spread in Europe and elsewhere. Held on Good Friday, generally from noon to three, the devotion normally includes sermons and meditations. After Franz Josef Haydn set the last words to music in 1786, other composers did the same: for instance, Charles Gounod in 1855, César Frank in 1859, and much more recently, Sir James MacMillan on commission from the BBC in 1994.

SACRED MUSIC

Resources from music that are available for retreatants making the Third Week of the Exercises embrace historical and contemporary compositions. Over the centuries, composers of Christian music have revealed a special sensitivity to the tragic beauty of the passion and crucifixion. Grief for the suffering of the Blessed Virgin Mary prompted many settings for the medieval sequence *Stabat Mater* ("At the cross her station keeping"). Giovanni Pierluigi da Palestrina (d. 1594) composed settings for the Lamentations of Jeremiah, while his younger friend Tomás Luis de Victoria created Tenebrae Responsories—both compositions still frequently sung on Good Friday.

The passion oratorios of Johann Sebastian Bach, *St. Matthew Passion* (1727) and *St. John Passion* (1724), give supreme aesthetic expression to the heartbreaking beauty of the suffering and death of Christ our Savior. Bach has found worthy successors in the passion music of Sir John Tavener (d. 2013) and Sir James Macmillan (b. 1959). Macmillan's *St. John Passion* (2008) and *St. Luke Passion* (2013) have led thousands into a deeper sense of solidarity with Christ in his passion and death. So, too, has *The War Requiem* of Benjamin Britten (d. 1976), a work for choir and orchestra based on the texts of the Latin requiem Mass and the poems of Wilfrid Owen (who was killed at the end of World War I).

Many hymns can lend emotional force to the prayer of retreatants in the Third Week. They would include Paul Gerhardt's "O Sacred Head Sore Wounded" (wonderfully arranged by Bach), Samuel Crossman's "My Song Is Love Unknown," and Isaac Watts's "When I Survey the Wondrous Cross."

PAINTING AND SCULPTURE

Christian artists repeatedly return to the task of representing through painting and sculpture the passion and death of Christ. Their works constantly serve to promote a deep compassion with him in his sufferings—the key, spiritual "fruit" of the Third Week for Ignatius.

A London exhibition presented at the National Gallery in the year 2000 and visited by 350,000 people (and several million in its BBC film version), "Seeing Salvation,"[5] featured masterpieces of all kinds from known and anonymous artists. To judge from the overwhelmingly silent visitors, the image that touched them most was "The Bound Lamb" by Francisco de Zurbarán (d. 1664). A young, innocent lamb, with its feet firmly bound together and set against a dark background, symbolized the sacrifice of Christ "the Lamb of God." From the thirteenth century, compassion for the wounded Savior had moved more and more to center stage in Christian sensibility and in the sacred art that nourished that spirituality.

The catalogue of the National Gallery exhibition devoted a long chapter to "passion and compassion."[6] This chapter was followed by one on "Praying the Passion."[7] I do not know any pair of chapters that would more effectively accompany visually the dynamic of the Third Week of the Exercises.

Right into the current century, the call to present the suffering and crucified Jesus has been heard by Christian artists everywhere. One powerful result is "The Homeless Christ," a seven-feet-long bronze work by a Canadian sculptor, Timothy Schmalz. It was first installed in the grounds of Regis College, Toronto, in 2013. Other castings can now be found in Austin

(Texas), Chicago, Davidson (North Carolina), New York, Washington, DC, Rio de Janeiro, Antwerp, Bruges, Dublin, Glasgow, London, Madrid, Manchester, Trastevere (Rome), Capernaum (Holy Land), Singapore, Melbourne (Australia), and outside the Papal Office of Charities in Rome. The statue depicts Christ as a homeless person sleeping on a park bench and covered by a blanket. The blanket covers his face and hands. His feet are visible and, in them, the marks of the nails from the crucifixion. We see the crucified Jesus only minimally.

"The Homeless Christ" brings us Jesus who was tragically beautiful on the cross. He is now beautiful in his fellow sufferers, those who continue to be "in agony until the end of the world." The statue represents the vulnerable and marginalized in society, with whom Christ identified himself (Matt 25:31–46).

THE PASSION OF CHRIST IN LITERATURE

I do not know whether Schmalz has read Blaise Pascal (d. 1662), who famously summed up the enduring presence of the crucified Christ in the mystery of all human suffering: "He is in agony until the end of the world, and we must not sleep during that time."[8] To express Christ's worldwide presence in all who suffer, we could gloss Pascal and say, "Where there is suffering there is Christ (*ubi dolor ibi Christus*)." It is Christ who is constantly revealed on the cross of human pain: "Where there is the cross there is Christ (*ubi crux ibi Christus*)."

We quoted in chapter 7 a poem ("Ecce Homo") by David Gascoyne. It took the form of a contemporary reflection on and application of Pascal's words: "He is in agony to the end of the world, and we must not sleep during that time." Gascoyne wrote the poem during the Second World War. He knew and to some extent could factor in the horrendous sufferings that Stalin and Hitler had been inflicting on human beings. But the full extent of the evil perpetrated in the Holocaust were not yet known to Gascoyne. The tragic passion endured by millions in Mao's China, Cambodia under Pol Pot, and in the genocidal massacres in Rwanda and elsewhere still lay hidden in the near future. The agony continues currently in a world under threat from nuclear warfare, climate change, and the destruction of the earth. The faces of over sixty million refugees and asylum seekers show us hunger and poverty of every kind. Images that bring us the passion of Christ have not disappeared but only changed and relocated. They invite us not only to grieve with Christ in his passion but also to grieve and act for a suffering world and a suffering planet.

So much literature can enrich our praying over the passion of Christ. Let me limit myself to two poems, the first being a subtle and laconic poem from the late thirteenth century that can set the mood for appropriate praying in the Third Week of the Exercises.

In this poem the speaker is a Christian who suffers with Mary as she keeps her lonely vigil at the foot of the cross. "Now goeth sun under wood. Me rueth, Mary, thy faire rode [face]. Now goeth sun under tree. Me rueth, Mary, thy Son and thee."[9] Sunset on Good Friday provides the setting for this poem.

The picture is drawn with economy and established in two stages. The sun is going down behind a/the "wood," which is then identified as the tree on which hangs the crucified Jesus. By repeating "Now" the poem evokes the moment when light drains out of the sky. We may shrink from seeing the light of day go, but we are powerless before a sunset. The passage of the sun suggests the irreversible dying and death of Jesus. Both his death and the onset of darkness seem inexorable.

Using a pun on "sun" (twice) and "Son" (once), the speaker grieves ("me rueth") over the suffering of Mary and her Son. The repetition of "me rueth" underlines the deep compassion felt by the speaker. As the sun goes down, he sees Mary's lovely face ("thy faire rode") lit up by the light of the setting sun. The pain on her fair face moves him and he grieves for this lovely lady and her dead Son.

This taut poem links the descent of the sun with the descent of Christ from the cross. The sun sinks below the horizon, just as Christ will sink from the cross into the arms of his Mother at the foot of the cross.

In July 2008, a highlight of World Youth Day in Sydney, Australia, came for many people with the Stations of the Cross that took them through the city to the crucifixion scene on the shore of the harbor as the sun was going down. On television millions followed that reenactment of the first Good Friday. Later, many more saw those Stations on DVD and heard the music, readings, and meditations that made them so religiously powerful.

In that presentation of the Stations of the Cross, the sun set just as Christ died and the chill of a winter's evening arrived. He was taken down from the cross, with darkness spreading across the gentle waves of Sydney harbor. The climax of those Stations of the Cross in 2008 proved a remarkable counterpart to the brief, thirteenth-century poem about Mary at the foot of the cross.

The death of Jesus against the background of a winter sunset over Sydney harbor invited us to remember the pain of that awful sunset in the life of Mary. Her love for Jesus went beyond anything we can imagine. Her pain at his death also went beyond our imaginings. But those stations of the cross in Sydney provided at least a little help toward picturing and sharing her pain.

The second poem, "The Good Thief Speaks" by Neville Braybrooke, appeared in *The Tablet* for March 29/April 5, 1997, and is reproduced with permission. By leaving out most punctuation, Braybrooke conveys a breathless sense of someone in great pain. Through elaborating the suffering of the good thief, the poet lets readers feel the suffering of Christ himself. Here and there, the poem goes beyond the Gospel narratives—not least by Mary relating to the good thief and then taking up Psalm 22 ("the crucifixion psalm") after her Son has uttered the first verse.

> The worst moment comes when they swing you up nailed
>   to the dead tree
> A blinding thud follows as they drop it into the earth
> Some say you have a black-out
> I shall know soon enough
> Trees should be places of song
>
> Now I am being swung upward
> The soldiers are pulling on the ropes

I am rising to meet my death
Then everything goes blank...

When I come round there is no singing to be heard
My bones are screaming with pain
Dogs are barking—but there are no robbers about
We stay clear of Jerusalem on days such as this

The man next to me speaks from time to time
He is thirsty
He cries out to his father in heaven
He asks mercy for those around him
Last night in the cells there were some who said he might
    be a king
I find myself urged to speak to him
I say "Remember me when you come into your kingdom"
In a clear voice he answers "You shall be there before the
    sun goes down"
I am struck silent by this promise
His words take away my last fear
Before night falls I shall be far away from this evil hill with
    its demons
I begin to feel like a bird about to be released into a sky
    without ending

My strength is slowly leaving me...

Below us are a group of patient women
There is one who has kept repeating "Never forget what
    my son has promised"
Sometimes she speaks as if she were praying—"Our fathers
    trusted in God and
he set them free"
What simple faith women have
My own mother died many years ago
Now I have another—O Lady in the Blue Cloak protect and
    watch over me

It is getting harder to breathe
My tongue sticks in my dry mouth...

Yesterday nobody came to the prison
No one cared
Yet this man beside me cares
I should like to kneel at his feet
But I cannot move

It is 3 o'clock and the sun has left the sky
Darkness is everywhere

Then suddenly I realize I am no longer nailed to a dead tree
I have only to stretch out my hands and they will be taken

FOURTH WEEK

11

THE RESURRECTION OF JESUS

This chapter, after taking up Christ's descent to the underworld and then his appearance to his Mother, turns to the consolation and joy shared by the risen Jesus. It will comment on the minimal place of the Holy Spirit in the Exercises and suggest some points from the four Gospels for contemplating the resurrection.

THE DESCENT TO THE DEAD

The very first preamble to the first contemplation of the Fourth Week reminds retreatants that Christ descended "into Hell, and from there he released the souls of the just" (SpEx 219; see 311). Here Ignatius modifies the traditional Western sense of Holy Saturday as a time of awesome silence when "our God sleeps," classically expressed by Johann Sebastian Bach at the end of his *St. Matthew Passion*: "*ruhe sanft, sanfte Ruh* (rest gently, gently rest)."

In the Eastern view of Christ in the underworld, immediately after his death and before Easter Sunday he was thoroughly active. Already victorious over death, he was engaged with liberating Adam, Eve, and innumerable others. Ignatius respected the active, Eastern sense of Holy Saturday when the triumphant Christ delivered the dead waiting for him in the "limbo of the fathers [*limbus partum*]." But, beyond this reverent nod toward an

Eastern view of Holy Saturday, Ignatius had nothing more to say about Christ's descent to the dead.

Nevertheless, we should add that any difference here between Eastern and Western Christianity was blurred by the time of Ignatius. The descent of Christ as the "harrowing of hell" had become a popular theme for Western art and drama in the Middle Ages. In *Piers Plowman*, William Langland (d. ca. 1400) portrayed Jesus as a beautiful young knight who faced combat with the Devil and Death. Seemingly defeated, he was in fact triumphant: "for Jesus had jousted well." In radiant light he then descended to the underworld, bound Satan with chains, and liberated Adam, Eve, and all those waiting to be brought up from the depths to heaven.[1]

In Western medieval plays and art, Christ often makes the cross the weapon with which he "harrows hell"—that is to say, defeats the powers of evil and releases their prisoners. At times he carries a lance, but it is a lance with a pennant showing a red cross.

By the time of Ignatius, Albrecht Dürer's woodcut of *Christ in Limbo* (1510) had gone around Europe. Unlike Eastern icons of Christ on Holy Saturday, it shows several devils trying in vain to impede Christ's redeeming work in the underworld.

Worship published in 2022 an article in which I translate with commentary a homily on Christ's descent to the *limbus partum* attributed to Epiphanius of Salamis and used for the Divine Office on Holy Saturday. About 10 percent of the complete homily deals with the descent of Christ, and that is the section that I translate. This section centers on Christ's dramatic meeting with Adam, when Christ explains how through his suffering he has more than reversed the evil committed by our first parents.

This ancient presentation of the descent to the dead is developed through a series of such binary contrasts as death/life, asleep/being awake, silence/speech, darkness/light, prison/freedom, underworld/heaven, the tree in Eden and the tree of the cross, and the sword guarding the way to the tree of life and the sword that pierced Christ's side. Those drawn to incorporate the descent into the Spiritual Exercises might find fruitful points in my article.[2]

THE APPEARANCE TO THE
BLESSED VIRGIN MARY

Ignatius opens the Fourth Week with the contemplation of a first appearance of the risen Christ to his blessed Mother (SpEx 219–20, 299). Although the Easter chapters of the Gospels do not report this appearance, it has a long pedigree in Christian tradition.[3] The earliest example comes from the so-called *Gospel of the Twelve Apostles*, which probably dates from the second century. In the same century, Tatian found the appearance to Mary in one of the canonical Gospels, when he turned Mary Magdalene of John 20:11–18 into Christ's own Mother.

In Eastern Christianity two decisive influences were St. Romanos the Singer, an outstanding sixth-century poet who introduced *kontakia*, or a new form of canticle, into the Byzantine liturgy, and the ninth-century metropolitan, St. George of Nicodemia. In his hymn "Mary at the Cross," Romanos has Christ saying to her from the cross, "Be of good courage, Mother; you will be the first to see me leave the tomb." In a homily, George portrays Mary as waiting at her Son's tomb from Good Friday evening until he appears to her in blazing glory on Easter morning.

In the fourth century, St. Ambrose of Milan, St. Ephrem, and St. endorsed the belief that Mary was the first to see Jesus after his resurrection from the dead. Ambrose symbolically "justified" this belief by linking the tomb from which Jesus rose with the Virgin's womb from which he had been born. The Western author who popularized a post-resurrection encounter between Christ and his Mother was Pseudo-Bonaventura, an anonymous thirteenth-century writer. His *Mirror of the Blessed Life of Jesus Christ* touchingly described an appearance to Mary. We also find the appearance to Mary affirmed in *The Life of Christ* by Ludolph of Saxony and the *Golden Legend* by James of Voragine (both of which Ignatius read during his convalescence in Loyola).

On his pilgrimage to Jerusalem, Ignatius may well have visited a chapel in Jerusalem in which legend placed the appearance to Mary. At Easter in Spain, a man representing Christ and a woman representing his Mother used to come in procession to meet and reenact the first post-resurrection appearance. Ignatius most probably knew that custom.

He may also have seen artistic representations of the scene like that of an altar piece created by Rogier van der Weyden around 1438 for Juan II of Castile. Various artistic expressions of Mary's role in the Easter events were already found in Spain. Rogier's masterpiece influenced subsequent Spanish versions of Christ appearing to his Mother—including that found on an altarpiece created by a group of artists for Isabella of Castile. On the popular artistic side, from the fifteenth into the sixteenth century, German woodcuts often portrayed Christ appearing to and blessing his Mother, who kneels in prayer. These woodcuts, which enjoyed a wide circulation, supported the private devotion and prayer of many individuals.

In proposing for prayer an encounter with Mary as Christ's first post-resurrection appearance, Ignatius was standing in a long tradition. After the seventeenth century the episode more or less disappeared from Christian art. Here and there the appearance continues in paraliturgical practices. In the Philippines, for instance, at dawn on Easter Sunday the ceremony of *Salubong* still celebrates the risen Christ's meeting with his Mother. A child dressed like an angel removes the veil that covers Mary's face; then children throw flowers on Jesus and Mary. In Spain the first appearance is commemorated by a procession of the risen Jesus and a procession of his Mother, which meet in front of the church.

The role expressed by Ignatius's proposed appearance to Mary has its place in the Easter week of the Spiritual Exercises. She certainly has her place in the total paschal experience, which runs from the crucifixion to the outpouring of the Holy Spirit. John's Gospel places her at the foot of the cross, where she suffers an unendurable loss (John 19:25–27). When the Church is about to be formed and fashioned through the gift of the Holy Spirit, Mary is there praying with Jesus' followers as they wait for Pentecost (Acts 1:14). To deny her a place in the paschal mystery would be to ignore the voices of John and Luke.

Christ the Consoler

In the obvious highlight of Ignatius's presentation of the resurrection, he writes of Christ our Lord fulfilling "the office of consoler." Ignatius knows that "Consoler" is not precisely, as such, a title given to Jesus by the New Testament. But the farewell discourse and prayer of Jesus supply ample reason for using this title (John 13:31—17:26), right from his words "do not let your hearts be troubled" (John 14:1). Probably recalling John 15:15 ("I have called you friends"), Ignatius invites retreatants to "draw comparisons with the way friends are accustomed to console one another" (SpEx 224). Psalm 16, originally pitched as a prayer for admission to the temple, breathes the joy and consolation that should permeate the Fourth Week: "my heart is glad, and my soul rejoices. In your presence there is fullness of joy, at your right hand happiness forever" (Ps 16:9, 11).

Writing in 1536 to Teresa Rejadell, Ignatius describes most vividly what he means by consolation: "The one [lesson] the Lord gives is interior consolation, which casts out all disturbance and draws us into total love of the Lord....With this divine consolation, all hardships are ultimately pleasure, all fatigues rest. For anyone who proceeds with this interior fervor, warmth, and consolation, there is no load so great that it does not seem light to them."[4]

Christ shares his risen life and heavenly joy. Ignatius confidently asks retreatants to "feel gladness and to rejoice intensely over the great glory and joy of Christ our Lord" (SpEx 221), and "to rejoice in the great joy and gladness of Christ our Lord" (SpEx 229). Joy is a most significant spin-off from love. Or else we might say that joy is woven into the very texture of love: "where there is love, there is joy (*ubi amor, ibi gaudium*)." Joy features firmly in the parable of the prodigal son (Luke 15:23, 24, 32), which would be better named "the parable of the merciful, loving father."

The Holy Spirit

At this point some may wonder whether Ignatius has moved the role of consoler away from the Holy Spirit. They might cite

"The Golden Sequence" (*Veni Sancte Spiritus*), composed in the thirteenth century either by Pope Innocent III or Cardinal Stephen Langton, the Archbishop of Canterbury, and used as the Sequence for Pentecost Sunday. Its third verse runs, "*Consolator optime, dulcis hospes animae, dulce refrigerium* (best consoler, sweet guest of the soul, sweet refreshment)."

Ignatius includes "the sixth appearance" of the risen Jesus (John 20:19–23), when the Lord gifts the disciples with the Holy Spirit (SpEx 304). A little further on, Ignatius notes how, before the ascension, Christ tells the apostles to wait in Jerusalem for the Holy Spirit (SpEx 312). The Spirit is not totally absent from the Spiritual Exercises. But should we expect a greater role for the Holy Spirit in the Exercises?[5]

Throughout the Exercises, the Blessed Virgin Mary regularly takes first place in the triple colloquy. The Gospels attribute her conception of Jesus to the action of the Holy Spirit (Matt 1:20; Luke 1:35). The Acts of the Apostles present her as being present in Jerusalem when the followers of Jesus prayed together for the outpouring of the Holy Spirit (Acts 1:14). Retreatants could, if they feel so drawn by God, join prayer to the Holy Spirit when they prayerfully commune with Mary.

Possibilities for Prayer

The Gospels of Matthew, Mark, Luke, and John are rich in possibilities for contemplation in the concluding Fourth Week of the Exercises.

The Easter chapter of Matthew offers at least four points for contemplation. (1) Mary Magdalene and another disciple called Mary go to the tomb of Jesus "after the sabbath, at the dawning of the first day of the week" (28:1). This verse recalls 4:16: "The people who sat in darkness have seen a great light, and for those who sat in the region of death light has dawned." The Light of the world appears at the dawn of a day when the sun will never set.

(2) The focus switches from the two women (27:61), to the guards set at the tomb by the high priests and Pharisees (27:62–66), to the women (28:1), to the guards (28:4), to the women (28:5–10), and back to the guards (28:11–15). The guards seem to

exercise all the power, but a glorious angel of the Lord descends to alter the whole situation. The guards are deeply shaken and become like dead men—something deeply ironical as they were stationed at the tomb to prevent any wrongdoing with the corpse of Jesus. The women feel "fear and great joy" (28:8). Faced with the revelation of the resurrection of Jesus and the beginning of the end of the world, fear is a proper human reaction, but joy must have the last word, that "great joy" which the Magi experienced when they reached the Christ Child (2:10).

J. R. R. Tolkien seems to have had in mind this reaction of the two women when in *The Lord of the Rings* he describes the reaction of the friends of Gandalf to the unexpected return of the old wizard: "between wonder, joy, and fear they stood and found no words to say."

(3) In the course of his ministry other people go to meet Jesus, for instance, the centurion (8:5). Easter Sunday proves the only time when Jesus goes to "meet" others: namely, Mary Magdalene and the other Mary (28:9). Now all the disciples belong as "brothers and sisters" to his new family of God (28:10).

(4) Before receiving the great commission on the mountain, the disciples both "worship" and "doubt" (28:17). But Jesus draws near them and assures them of his presence and comprehensive authority: over "heaven and earth" and "all nations." He will be with them "all days," even "to the end of time."

In Mark's Easter story (16:1–8), God is never explicitly mentioned but is made known through what happens in Jesus' resurrection from the dead. There are three contrasts built into the account: darkness/light, absence/presence, and silence/speech. First, God has overcome darkness and death; the stone that closes the tomb "has been rolled away," and one understands it to have been rolled away by God. Second, the body is not there in the tomb, but an angel (represented as "the young man" robed in white) mediates Jesus' presence. Third, the confident words of the angel to Mary Magdalene and her two female companions take a tripartite form: to begin with, the great truth ("he was raised"); then a reference to the setting of the tomb itself ("he is not here"); and lastly, a statement about the precise niche where Jesus had been buried ("see the place where they laid him").

The dramatic, numinous moment of God's self-revelation prompts awed wonder, silence, and even fear. The male disciples had been "utterly astounded" (6:51) when Jesus walked to their boat across the water. Now the three women flee in fear from the tomb and remain silent until they can deliver the angel's message to the male disciples (16:8).

In the Fourth Week of the Exercises, the ascension is to be one of the contemplations, in fact, the final contemplation (SpEx 226). In SpEx 312, Ignatius cites Acts 1:1–12. But there is also a version of the ascension at the end of Luke's Gospel, which Ignatius fails to note but that fits excellently into the dynamic of the Exercises: "Then he led them out as far as Bethany, and, lifting up his hands, he blessed them. While he was blessing them, he withdrew from them, and was carried up into heaven. And they worshipped him, and returned to Jerusalem with *great joy*, and they were continually in the Temple blessing God" (Luke 24:50–52). There have been examples of prayer in Luke (such as the *Benedictus*, the *Magnificat*, and the *Nunc Dimittis*), as well as instructions about prayer, not least the shorter form of the Lord's Prayer. But after Luke's briefer account of the ascension, we hear for the first time of the disciples of Jesus praying and doing so "with great joy," the main fruit of the Fourth Week.

In John's first Easter chapter, the story of Mary Magdalene's encounter with the risen Jesus invites retreatants to enter prayerfully into the whole story and make it their own. Her lasting identity is bestowed on her through the love that Jesus has for her and the love that she has for him. The very names used ("Mary" and "Rabbouni") breathe love and suggest imaginatively hearing Jesus say our names to each of us. No one says our name as beautifully as the risen Jesus.[6]

John's second Easter chapter can work the same way in the Exercises. But here it is not Mary Magdalene but Peter being the disciple loved and consoled. Through his meeting with the risen Jesus, he, too, receives his permanent identity in life and death.

The Easter narratives of the Four Gospels offer rich material for prayer as we reflect on appearances to the Mother of Jesus, Mary Magdalene, Simon Peter, the eleven apostles, and other individuals and groups. Those doing the Exercises might do what Ignatius suggests elsewhere (for the nativity, for example)—move beyond being mere observers and insert themselves actively into these Easter stories. This can help prepare them for what follows in the Contemplation for Attaining Love.

12

THE CONTEMPLATION FOR ATTAINING LOVE

The Contemplation for Attaining Love (SpEx 230–37), while somewhat free-floating in the text of the Spiritual Exercises, normally finds its place as the crown of the Fourth Week.[1] It is not that the theme of love has been absent earlier in the Exercises. Love already features at the start of the Second Week in the contemplations on the Call of the Earthly King (SpEx 97) and the Incarnation (SpEx 104), and even earlier in the fifteenth annotation (SpEx 15). Now Ignatius proposes seeking the grace of loving God as generously as possible, to draw together the central dynamic of the Exercises for those who have completed the four weeks.

After examining two aspects of love that Ignatius emphasizes, we reflect on the grace to which this contemplation aspires and take up four points he puts forward. We conclude by adding two further considerations on love.

LOVE IN DEEDS AND LOVE AS COMMUNICATION

In his opening note, Ignatius lines up with a central New Testament theme: "Love finds its expression in deeds more than in words" (SpEx 230). Love entails practical action to advance the welfare of others. In the words of John's Gospel, "God so loved the world that he gave his only begotten Son" (John 3:16). In Luke's Gospel, the parable of the prodigal son (15:11–32) never speaks of "love" either as noun or verb, but the story would remain unintelligible unless we recognize how the father acts by giving himself in love to both his sons. His particular love for his younger son does not express itself merely through gifts like clothing, a ring, and a family feast (Luke 15:22–23). It is the father's active self-gift to the returning prodigal that transforms the situation and loves his son back into life (Luke 15:20).

In a classic passage Paul personifies love and sixteen times introduces different verbs, all with an active meaning and in the present tense (1 Cor 13:4–8a). Love consists in actions that occur when love does certain things or actively refrains from doing other things. For Paul love is verbal, a constant performance.[2]

The "more than" in Ignatius's maxim ("love finds its expression in deeds more than in words") implies that love is also found in words. The beauty of Paul's tribute to love in 1 Corinthians is proof, if any is needed, that love also finds its expression in words. The *Confessions* of St. Augustine (see chapter 4 above) witnesses to the love conveyed in words that distinguishes many classical authors of Christianity. Once we move beyond spiritual to secular literature, we meet innumerable verbal expressions of love in lyric poetry, great novels, and dramas of many cultures.

Nowadays films have become major players in social commentary. Once again they need not appeal explicitly to "love" when they wish to express it. *In the Heat of the Night* presents the deep respect and affection that grows between a white sheriff in Mississippi (Rod Steiger) and a visiting black detective from Philadelphia (Sidney Poitier) who helps to solve a local murder. When the detective finally leaves by train, the words of a not-very-articulate sheriff show how the experience of working together has banished ugly, racist prejudices and triggered a change of heart: "Virgil [Sidney Poitier], you take care."

Ignatius's second conviction about love is that it consists in "mutual communication" or giving and receiving. Here he puts forward an "inclusion," or reintroduction of a theme enunciated at the start of the Spiritual Exercises. Back in Annotation 15

Ignatius had declared it "more opportune and much better that the Creator and Lord should *communicate* himself to the faithful soul...as he inflames her in his love and praise." The director of the Exercises should "leave the Creator to work directly with the creature and the creature with the Creator and Lord" (SpEx 15).

This "giving" and "receiving" can be identified, respectively, with "the love of "benevolence (*amor benevolentiae*)" and "the love of desire (*amor concupiscentiae*)." We can also speak, respectively, of the Creator's altruistic or descending love (*agapē*) and the creature's ascending or receptive love (*erōs*). In his encyclical of December 25, 2005, *Deus Caritas Est* (God Is Love), Pope Benedict XVI declared it to be in accordance with "the true nature of love" that the two "find a proper unity in the one reality of love." For "anyone who wishes to give must also receive love" (*Deus Caritas Est*, 7).

Apropos of the divine giving, one should add, as Annotation 15 implies, that in lovingly bestowing on us what is good and valuable, God comes with the gift. All divine giving is self-giving. The "agapeic" activity that flows in spontaneous abundance from the divine goodness communicates nothing less than the divine reality. Dionysius the Pseudo-Areopagite (who would more accurately be called Pseudo-Dionysius the Areopagite) disseminated the theme, "*bonum diffusivum sui*," the good—above all, the divine Good—shares itself (*Divine Names*, 4). Often called "gift-love," this divine *agapē* would be more accurately styled the "self-gift-of-love."

Mutual communication strikingly characterizes the public ministry of Jesus. All four Gospels show Jesus as thoroughly receiver-centered in his mode of communication. He did not treat his audience as passive hearers to whom special information about God could simply be committed. Rather, he took seriously their circumstances and reactions. He shared freely, and his listeners could freely respond or refuse to respond. The parable of sowing the seed (Mark 4:3–9) classically expressed this aspect of Jesus' communicative activity.

His miracles of healing meant much more than mere acts of kindness toward sick and disabled persons. They belonged to an open invitation to respond to his activity and let his powerful presence make new sense of their human and religious situation. Some groups, such as the people of Chorazin and Bethsaida, missed the point of these events and failed to integrate his miraculous actions into the way they read off their world and responded to God (Matt 11:20–24; Luke 10:13–15).

There is, of course, a startling paradox in naming Jesus "The Great Communicator." From the normal perspective of communication studies, he proved himself almost a total failure. After an initial success, he was misunderstood and abandoned by the large crowds he first attracted. The core group of disciples could not fathom his warnings about his coming fate and, at his arrest, almost all fled in terror. A few individuals did better at receiving and interpreting his meaning: an army officer (Matt 8:5–10), certain women whom he had healed (Luke 8:2–3), and perhaps some children (Matt 21:15). According to Mark, it was only after the crucifixion that someone finally grasped the secret of Jesus' real identity: "Truly this man was the Son of God" (Mark 15:39). With his resurrection and sending of the Holy Spirit, Jesus' power to communicate dramatically changed. But during his earthly ministry he failed or at least appeared to have largely failed as a communicator.

THE GRACE OF THIS CONTEMPLATION

Key Ignatian terms permeate the grace desired from this contemplation. Asking "for what I want...will be to ask for *interior knowledge* of all the good I have received so that *acknowledging* this with gratitude, I may be able to *love and serve* his Divine Majesty in everything" (SpEx 233; italics mine).

The language of "interior knowledge" turns up early in the Exercises. Ignatius proposes that the retreatants should pray for "an interior knowledge" of their sins and "an abhorrence of them" (SpEx 63). This language carries a richly positive meaning when retreatants pray for an "interior knowledge of the Lord who became human for me" (SpEx 104).[3] This in-depth knowing arises in and through love; it resembles the grace that Paul prays for: "May your love abound more and more in knowledge and every insight, so that you may discern what really matters" (Phil 1:9).

Acknowledging with gratitude "all the good I have received" is clearly an exercise that brings the memory into play. In fact, Ignatius goes on at once to instruct retreatants to "bring to *memory* the benefits received—creation, redemption, and particular gifts—pondering with great affection how much God Our Lord has done for me, and how much he has given me of what He has" (SpEx 234; italics mine).

Reference to the three powers of the soul (memory, intellect, and will) and, in particular, to memory, threads its way through the Contemplation for Attaining Love (SpEx 230–37).[4] Point one closes with the prayer that begins, "Take, Lord, and receive all my liberty, my *memory*, my *understanding*, and my entire *will*" (SpEx 234). Ignatius cites here "the three powers of the soul," even if, unlike the heading for the first exercise of the First Week, they are not brought together and called "the three powers" (SpEx 45). In the Contemplation for Attaining Love, "my entire will" is stressed by being preceded by the offering of "all my liberty." "Understanding" is preceded by equivalents, "pondering with great affection how much God our Lord has done for me" and reflecting and considering "within myself what, in all reason and justice, I ought for my part to offer and give to his Divine Majesty."[5] Point one has opened with work for "my memory"; I should "bring to mind the benefits received—creation, redemption, and particular gifts" (SpEx 234).

Here the benefits to remember include that of being redeemed, which implies being delivered *from* various evils, including the burden and guilt of my own sins, as well as being delivered *for* various blessings, above all, eternal life with God. Praying for an "interior knowledge of all the good I have received" (SpEx 233) also entails praying to know truly the blessing of being forgiven my sins and being saved from their burden. Memory should cover the benefits of forgiveness and healing, as well as such gifts as God's dwelling in all creatures (SpEx 235).

MEMORY RECALLS GIFTS
AND HEALS THE PAST

Ignatius assigns a double role to memory, the first power of the soul, in what comes in the First Week of the Exercises and in the Contemplation for Attaining Love (placed after the Fourth Week). I suggest that John 21 functions as a rich source for illuminating biblically that double role.[6] The chapter suggests what the disciples of Jesus have experienced in the last three or four years, since their initial call in chapter 1. (1) Extraordinary benefits already conferred are recalled (and expanded), as well as (2) past sins being evoked and forgiven.

(1) The Memory of Benefits

John's closing chapter opens by announcing that it will describe how the risen Jesus "manifested himself again" to the disciples, in fact to Peter and six other disciples (John 21:1–2). The "again" suggests the unique graces of the earlier Easter appearances: to Mary Magdalene (John 20:11–18), to the disciples minus Thomas (John 20:19–23), and to the disciples including Thomas (John 20:24–29).[7]

The choice of the verb *manifest* echoes a much earlier benefit in John's Gospel where we read of Jesus changing water into wine at a marriage feast: "This, the first of his signs, Jesus did at Cana in Galilee, and manifested his glory; and his disciples believed in him" (John 2:11). The Johannine narrative encourages the reader to remember that episode, by noting that one of the six fishermen who join Peter for a night out on Lake Tiberias is Nathanael, who comes "from Cana in Galilee" (John 21:2). Just as Galilee saw Jesus working his first sign to manifest his glory, so now the same Galilee witnesses a new gift: the risen Jesus manifesting himself as "the Lord" (John 21:7, 12).

Jesus does so "just as day is breaking" (John 21:4). He is there on the beach when dawn comes and the darkness slips away. The scene evokes a past blessing: the cure of a blind man (John 9:1–41) and Jesus' self-revelation, "I am the Light of the world" (John 9:5).

The spring dawn at the end of the Gospel recalls the Gospel's very beginning and the Light that shines in the darkness to enlighten and give life to every man and woman (John 1:4-9).

In the closing chapter of John the seven disciples have fished all night without catching anything. Now the stranger on the lakeside tells them to cast their net on the right side of the boat. They do so and make an enormous catch (John 21:6, 8, 11). This suggests the gift of "life in abundance" (John 10:10), which, right from its prologue, the Gospel has promised that the Light of the world will bring (John 1:4).

The extraordinary catch of fish, the only miraculous or semi-miraculous this-worldly event in the Easter chapters of the four Gospels, recalls the multiplication of the loaves *and fishes* (John 6:1-15). In the discourse that follows that miracle, Jesus spoke of people being "hauled [*helkuō*]" to him (John 6:44), a verb that turned up later in the promise: "When I am lifted up from the earth, I will haul all people to myself" (John 12:32). Now in the closing chapter of John, the same verb recurs when Peter hauls ashore the unbroken net containing 153 large fish. Symbolically, Peter the fisherman is engaged in the work of hauling others to the Lord.

When the disciples reach land, they see that Jesus has already prepared for them some fish and bread (John 21:9). Jesus' words and gestures recall what he has done and then promised when multiplying the loaves and fishes for the five thousand (John 6:8-11). Asking the disciples to fetch him some of the fish they have just caught and adding them to the fish he has already prepared, he "takes" and "gives" them bread and fish (John 21:10,13). We are asked to remember his "taking" and "giving" to a large crowd during his earthly ministry (John 6:11) and his promise that those who come to him "will not hunger" (John 6:35). "The Son of Man will *give* you food that endures for eternal life" (John 6:27); he promises that "the food that I will *give* for the life of the world is my flesh" (John 6:51). By evoking John 6, John 21 recalls the wonderful gift of the Eucharist. As the host at breakfast, Jesus resurrects what he has done and promised as host during his lifetime—on the shore of the same Lake Tiberias. It is only in the Fourth Gospel that this lake is called the Lake of Tiberias (John 6:1 and 21:1)—a detail that significantly holds together chapter 6 and chapter 21.

Thus John 21 brings back to mind many benefits already received, right from chapter 1. Sometimes this happens with deft brevity. When Jesus first met Peter, (a) he called him by his original name "Simon, son of John" and at once, (b) without providing an explanation, indicated the grace of a new function: "you will be called Cephas (which is translated Peter)" (John 1:42). Now at the end, Jesus (a) speaks to Peter three times as "Simon, son of John," and (b) commissions him to feed "my lambs" and "my sheep" (John 21:15–17). Peter's commission will call him to martyrdom in the service of the Lord's flock (John 21:18–19).

Like Philip at the beginning of John's Gospel (John 1:43), Peter at the end receives again a call. It is the simple, radical, and uniquely grace-filled call to faithful discipleship: "follow me" (John 21:19, 22).

During his earthly lifetime, to enable their spiritual growth, Jesus put questions to various individuals and groups (for example, John 1:38; 2:4) and, not least, the question to the Twelve, "Do you also wish to go away?" Peter answered magnificently: "Lord, to whom shall we go? You have the words of eternal life" (John 6:67–68). Chapter 21 recalls Jesus' habit of asking disturbing and grace-conferring questions and features this habit in an intensified way. When asking Peter "do you love me?," Jesus does so three times—making it the only question he ever repeats verbatim in the entire Gospel (John 21:15–17).

This way of looking at John 21 accounts for the deeply haunting quality that many readers find in it. It brings back to mind such wonderful benefits already received as the self-manifestation of the risen Christ, the gift of the Eucharist, and the call to faithful discipleship in the service of the Lord's flock. The text recalls past graces that can touch us again.

(2) Sinful Failures

The memory exercised by John 21 also allows a broken past to resurface, be healed, and form a basis for a new future. The "charcoal fire" (John 21:9) around which the disciples take their breakfast points back to an earlier charcoal fire in the high priest's courtyard, the scene where Peter three times denied his Master (John 18:18). The memory of this abject failure is reinforced by the triple denial now matched by Peter's triple affirmation of his love for Jesus. Peter must acknowledge his sin and receive forgiveness before he begins a pastoral ministry that will eventually lead to his martyrdom.

What should not pass unnoticed is the way the lakeside breakfast recalls earlier meals in John's narratives, meals that should be remembered not only with gratitude but also with shame and sorrow. They have been occasions of deadly threats against Jesus and Lazarus (John 12:1–11), disputes (John 12:4–8), betrayal (John 13:21–30), and misunderstanding (John 2:3–4). The meal at which five thousand people were miraculously fed was followed by the discourse on the bread of life, which ends with many disciples leaving Jesus and the first warning of Judas's treacherous betrayal (John 6:25–71). The last chapter of John does explicitly recall the Last Supper (John 21:20). But the Easter meal at dawn serves to recall and heal several *other* meals and crises, mainly sinful crises, associated with them.

(3) Exercitants and John 21

John 21 forms a tissue of memories for Peter and the other six disciples, memories of graces received and sins committed. That makes it a rich biblical resource for those doing the Spiritual Exercises, especially when Ignatius invites them to exercise their memory in the First Week and later in the Contemplation for Attaining Love. For them as well, John 21 will bring up memories of Jesus and past encounters with him, memories that concern past benefits and past failures.

This way of looking at John 21 accounts for the deeply haunting quality which many readers find in it. It brings back to mind such wonderful benefits already received as the self-manifestation of the risen Christ, the gift of the Eucharist, and the call to faithful discipleship in the service of the Lord's flock. The text recalls past graces which can touch us again.

Both during the Spiritual Exercises and in other contexts, bringing back to the surface grateful and painful memories can become a rich occasion of grace. Memory can provide the start for a fresh future—through the loving and forgiving presence of the risen Lord.

CONCLUDING REMARKS

I have dwelt on the place of memory in the Contemplation for Attaining Love and recommended John 21 as a superb biblical support for this contemplation. The grace Ignatius proposes here is that of being enabled to "love and serve" God. This not only picks up again Annotation 15 and its call to love, praise, and serve God (SpEx 15) but also joins John 21 in its language of the love that binds Peter and the beloved disciple to Jesus (John 21:15–19, 20) as they remember past graces and failures.

The famous prayer "Take, Lord, receive [*Suscipe*]" asks at the end, "Give me the grace to love you, for that is enough for me" (SpEx 234). This matches the grace prayed for, that "I may be able to love and serve his Divine Majesty" (SpEx 233).[8]

The further points for prayer, points 2 and 3, aim at focusing love through the marvelous way God "dwells in creatures"—in the nonliving "elements, giving them being, in the plants, causing them growth, in the animals, producing sensation....He makes a temple of me, as I have been created in the likeness and image of his Divine Majesty " (SpEx 235). Highlighting the universal presence of God, Ignatius sees every creature as a dwelling place of God, who brings about their characteristic activities.

Point 3 makes this vision of the created universe more personal, by recalling that "God works and labors *on my behalf* in all created things on the face of the earth" (SpEx 236; italics mine). Like the encyclical of Pope Francis, *Laudato Si'* (May 24, 2015), Ignatius encourages a positive, proper care for our common home, the planet earth. God has blessed us abundantly through the created context in which we human beings all live. It is not to be judged and treated simply by its utility for me or for us.

Ignatius sums up his appreciation of what the Creator has done for us by employing two images in point 4, to encourage retreatants to see how "all that is good and every gift descends from on high...as rays descend from the sun, and waters from a fountain" (SpEx 237). This is to apply to the infinitely generous love of God images of the sun and a fountain taken from the Scriptures. Jesus spoke of divine love in terms of the sun rising on all human beings alike (Matt 5:45). John's Gospel brings in the image of "rivers of living water" flowing from the side of Jesus (John 7:37–39).

The Scriptures may remind us that Ignatius does not pretend to offer an exhaustive account of love, whether divine or human. Let me give two examples of further themes about love that could find a place in the Contemplation for Attaining Love.

First, John's Gospel appreciates how the eyes of love see the truth (20:8; 21:7). The language of Ephesians 1:18 about "the eyes of the heart being enlightened" encouraged Christian theologians, from Augustine to Karl Rahner and Bernard Lonergan, to endorse the principle classically enunciated by Richard of St. Victor (d. 1173): "*ubi amor ibi oculus* (where love [exists] there is vision)."[9]

Second, a widely beloved passage from the Song of Songs embodies the desire of all faithful love to prove eternal (8:6–7). As a lyric of Irving Berlin puts it, "I'll be loving you always." By its very nature, love aspires to be everlasting.

At the end of the material on the Contemplation for Attaining Love, Ignatius moves at once to expound "three ways of praying" (SpEx 238–60). The second of these consists in contemplating slowly the meaning of some prayers (SpEx 249–57), one of which is found in the New Testament (the Our Father) and another draws on Luke's Gospel (the Hail Mary). Earlier Ignatius has very briefly mentioned reading the Gospels (SpEx 100). At these points in the Spiritual Exercises, he approaches the method of *lectio divina*. We will come to *lectio divina* in the first appendix.

APPENDIX I

THE HISTORY AND PRACTICE OF
LECTIO DIVINA

Early in 2020 Paulist Press published *The New Testament with Lectio Divina*.[1] In the advertising material, the press explained this traditional, monastic practice as follows: "*Lectio Divina* is a way of praying the Scriptures that uniquely opens our heart to the Lord. With this prayer we enter the Scriptures personally, allowing the original context to touch our everyday lives, lead us to prayer, and call us to action." Such "reflective reading of scripture," Paulist Press added, "has long been a popular devotional practice in the Church from the earliest centuries."

This appendix will set itself to do four things: provide some historical background to *lectio divina* ("divine reading"); set out at length how Vatican II retrieved this practice, including the very use of the term *lectio divina*; recall how *lectio divina* was received in papal and other teaching and practice (such as by Pope Benedict XVI, Ernesto Cardenal, and Carlo Maria Martini); and end by summarizing the practice and a few examples of *lectio divina*.

HISTORICAL ORIGINS

An ancient, fascinating letter written by an Egyptian Christian, Bishop Theonas of Alexandria, recommends what he calls the sacred study of the Sacred Scriptures and what we would call *lectio divina*. He urges a young officer (Lucianus) of the emperor to engage in a daily, meditative reading of the Scriptures; it will "feed the soul" and "enrich the mind":

> Let no day pass by without reading some portion of the Sacred Scriptures, at such convenient hour as offers, and giving some space to meditation. And never cast off the habit of reading in the Holy Scriptures; for nothing feeds the soul and enriches the mind so well as those sacred studies do.[2]

Theonas wrote around 300 AD, almost fifty years after the death of a deeply biblical and very influential Christian writer, Origen (d. about 254).

Origen pioneered the method and terminology of *lectio divina* as a group and individual practice. In a letter to Gregory of Neo-Caesarea he wrote, "Diligently apply yourself to the reading of the sacred Scriptures...seek aright, and with unwavering trust in God... the meaning of holy Scriptures....Be not satisfied with knocking and seeking; for prayer is of all things indispensable to the knowledge of the things of God."[3] Origen encouraged his audience to read devoutly the Scriptures and allow themselves to be brought into the living presence of Christ, the Word to be found and savored in the words of all the inspired Scriptures, the books of both the Old and New Testament. Origen understood Christ to be incarnate in the Scriptures and so function as the interpretive key that unlocks their life-giving meaning and message.[4]

In the brief section devoted to *lectio divina*, a now-classic document of the Pontifical Biblical Commission recalled Origen's concern for "regular, even daily reading of Scripture" as a group practice: "He used to give homilies based on a text read continuously throughout a week...there were daily gatherings devoted to the reading and explanation of Scripture."[5]

After Origen, the prayerful reading of the Scriptures was referred to as *lectio divina* and *lectio sacra* by St. Ambrose of Milan, St. Augustine of Hippo, and St. Hilary of Poitiers. In the sixth century, St. Benedict of Nursia established the monastic practice of *lectio divina.* The motto *ora et labora* (pray and work) summarized the daily life in Benedictine monasteries: it consisted of liturgical prayer, manual work, and *lectio divina*, a slow reading of the Scriptures and prayerful pondering of their meaning. Chapter 48 of the *Rule of St Benedict* specified times and circumstances for *lectio divina.*[6]

In the twelfth century, Guigo II, a Carthusian monk and prior of the Grande Chartreuse, described and prescribed four stages in the practice of *lectio divina*: quiet reading (*lectio*), meditating on the text (*meditatio*), responding with prayer (*oratio*), and quiet stillness in God's presence (*contemplatio*).[7] In the sixteenth century St. John of the Cross taught his fellow Carmelites and others this fourfold scheme for practicing *lectio divina.*[8]

The monastic practice continued, but from the sixteenth century an aversion to *lectio divina* set in. Many Catholics lost confidence that the inspiring voice of the Spirit would speak to them through the prayerful reading of the Scriptures. Some feared that such personal reading could deteriorate into a one-sidedly private and divisive interpretation of biblical texts. The twentieth century, however, brought a retrieval of *lectio divina*, effected by Jean Leclercq,[9] among others, and officially endorsed by one constitution and several decrees of the Second Vatican Council (1962–65). That conciliar teaching decisively encouraged many priests, religious, seminarians, and lay persons to seek a relationship to God through a meditative reading of the Scriptures.

MODERN RECOMMENDATIONS

When four times recommending the practice of *lectio divina* in the Dogmatic Constitution on Divine Revelation (*Dei Verbum* 25), the Second Vatican Council does not here explicitly use the term *lectio divina* and remains silent about Origen and Benedict. But it cites Paul, Augustine of Hippo, Jerome, and Ambrose of Milan in support of the prayerful reading of the Bible.

First, all who are "officially engaged in the ministry of the Word, particularly priests, deacons or catechists must cling to the

Scriptures by unremitting sacred reading (*assidua lectione sacra*) and meticulous study."[10] Here Vatican II uses the ancient term *lectio sacra* rather than the equally ancient, largely equivalent *lectio divina*. A quotation from Augustine drives home this duty for the ministers of the Word: it must not happen that anyone "becomes an empty preacher of the Word of God to others, not being a hearer of the Word in his own heart."[11]

Second, the Council "vehemently and specifically exhorts all the Christian faithful, above all members of religious institutes, to learn 'the surpassing knowledge of Jesus Christ' (Phil 3:8) by frequent reading [*frequenti lectione*] of the divine Scriptures" (*Dei Verbum*, 25). A quotation from Jerome backs up this injunction: "ignorance of the Scripture is ignorance of Christ."[12] The maxim puts negatively a conviction found at the heart of the spirituality of Origen and his successors: prayerful knowledge of the Scriptures is knowledge of Christ.

Third, the same article 25 of *Dei Verbum* goes on to encourage all the faithful "to approach gladly the sacred text itself, whether through the sacred liturgy which is filled with divine utterances, or through devout reading (*per piam lectionem*)." So the reading of the divinely inspired and inspiring Scriptures should be not only "unremitting" and "frequent" but also "devout."

Fourth and finally, when exhorting the faithful to practice prayerful reading of the Scriptures, the same article cites Ambrose in its support: "Prayer should accompany the reading of Sacred Scripture, so that a dialogue takes place between God and human beings. We address God when we pray; we listen to him when we read the divine oracles." Such a reading of Scripture accompanied by prayer could serve as a concise definition of *lectio divina* or *lectio sacra*.

Jared Wicks has carefully traced the development of article 25 of the Dogmatic Constitution on Divine Revelation in which Vatican II retrieved and taught the devout and prayerful reading of the Scriptures no fewer than four times.[13] But this account is incomplete; several items need to be added.

First, we should go beyond article 25 to include the final article of *Dei Verbum* (26). It expressed the wish that both through regular study (*studio*) and prayerful reading (*lectione*) "of the sacred books," the divine revelation may "more and more fill the hearts of human beings." Just as "the life of the Church receives increase from constant attendance at the Eucharistic mystery," so "a new impulse of the spiritual life may be expected from an increased veneration of the Word of God" (*Dei Verbum*, 26). That veneration is to be shown not only through biblical studies but also through *lectio divina*. Thus in its concluding two articles, *Dei Verbum* five times exhorts Catholics and other Christians to practice *lectio divina*.

Second, like the Constitution on Divine Revelation, two other documents of Vatican II—one (*Perfectae Caritatis*, the Decree on the Up-to-date Renewal of Religious Life) promulgated shortly before *Dei Verbum* and the other (*Presbyterorum Ordinis*, the Decree on the Ministry and Life of Priests) promulgated less than three weeks after *Dei Verbum*—both include brief exhortations to engage in prayerful reading of the Scriptures.[14] The first decree instructed members of religious institutes "to draw on the genuine sources of Christian spirituality." To begin with, this means "having at hand the Sacred Scripture on a daily basis, so that they might learn 'the surpassing knowledge of Christ Jesus' (Phil 3:8) by reading (*lectione*) and meditating on (*meditatione*) the divine scriptures" (*Perfectae Caritatis* 6). The decree for priests took up this theme twice, once echoing what we have just seen in the decree for religious: "the sacred knowledge" of a priestly minister is "primarily drawn from the reading (*lectione*) and meditation (*meditatione*) of Sacred Scripture" (*Presbyterorum Ordinis*, 19). On the other occasion, the decree for priests introduced verbatim the term *lectio divina*: "in the light of a faith that has been nourished by divine reading (*lectione divina*), priests can diligently search for signs of God's will" (*Presbyterorum Ordinis* 18).[15] Thus, in a document promulgated at its last sitting, the Second Vatican Council accepted the term *lectio divina* to name what it expounded in *Dei Verbum* about the devout and prayerful reading of the Scriptures. And so for the first time the term, which over many centuries had already named this practice, was used by a general council of the Church.

Third, Wicks ended his article by praising *Dei Verbum* for inculcating "the practice of devout Bible reading," which can "rejuvenate church members." Thus, "Vatican II's dogmatic constitution *Dei Verbum* has a significant pastoral conclusion concerning what is today known as *lectio divina*."[16] But, it should be added, this ancient practice had been known and named as *lectio divina* (or *lectio sacra*) long before "today"—in fact, right back to Origen in the third century.

Fourth and finally, Wicks could also have noted how early articles in *Dei Verbum*, albeit again without naming it, evoke the experience of *lectio divina* to which the concluding two articles point. The prologue opens with what could be a succinct description of *lectio divina*—"hearing the Word of God devoutly" (DV 1)—which will be echoed in the final article, with its hope that "a new impulse of spiritual life may be expected from an increased veneration of the Word of God" (DV 26). The prologue quotes words from 1 John 1:2–3 that might be used by those engaged in communal *lectio divina*: "We announce to you what we have seen and heard."

When describing the experience of divine self-revelation as a personal encounter in which God "speaks to human beings as friends" (DV 2), *Dei Verbum* could also have been referring to the encounter with God to be experienced through *lectio divina*. The constitution reflects on the complete Christ-event when it invokes his "total" presence (DV 4). But that quality also characterizes the presence of the living Christ in liturgical celebration and *lectio divina*.

The Holy Spirit is at work, chapter 2 of the constitution emphasizes, when the faithful "grow in insight" into the realities "being transmitted," which obviously include the Sacred Scriptures. *Dei Verbum* cites "the contemplation and study of believers" who, like the Blessed Virgin Mary, "ponder these things in [their] heart." This growth in insight effected by the Spirit "comes from the intimate understanding of spiritual realities" that believers "experience." Such language also serves to describe what happens in and through the communal and personal practice of *lectio divina*. The closing words of article 8 likewise apply to what the Holy Spirit can bring about through *lectio divina*: "The Holy Spirit, through whom the living voice of the Gospel rings out in the Church...leads believers to all truth, and makes the word of Christ dwell in them abundantly (Col 3:16.)."

Whether or not the drafters of *Dei Verbum* noticed or intended this, what comes at the beginning (DV 1-2, 4 and 8) anticipates the substance of what is taught at the end about *lectio divina* (DV 25–26). It strengthens the case that Wicks argued if we recognize the presence of an "inclusion." What comes implicitly at the end of the constitution about *lectio divina* takes up and develops what we have already read at the beginning.

POST–VATICAN II RECEPTION

After the Second Vatican Council had, at least once explicitly, retrieved the term *lectio divina*, it slowly began to enter official teaching and related usage. In 1990 a major translation of Vatican II documents still felt constrained to render *"lectio divina"* as "the reading of God's word" (*Presbyterorum Ordinis* 18).[17] A 1999 translation of the conciliar documents followed Flannery in mistakenly rendering *"lectio divina"* as "spiritual reading."[18] But in 1993 the Pontifical Biblical Commission could list four headings under the "Use of the Bible": "In the Liturgy, *Lectio Divina*, In Pastoral Ministry, [and] In Ecumenism," before commending *lectio divina* in both its individual and communal forms.[19] The 1994 *Catechism of the Catholic Church* presented "the *lectio divina*, where the Word of God is so read and meditated that it becomes prayer," and is thus "rooted in the celebration of the liturgy of the hours."[20] Pope John Paul II's 1999 apostolic exhortation *Ecclesia in America* recalled that "the reading of the Bible, accompanied by prayer, is known in the tradition of the Church as *lectio divina*, and it is a practice to be encouraged among all Christians" (n. 31).

Finally, Benedict's XVI's 2010 apostolic exhortation *Verbum Domini* picked out seminarians and members of religious institutes as those whose lives and vocations should be nourished by *lectio divina*, understood as a practice related to but distinct from "biblical studies" (82–83). *Verbum Domini* pressed on to recommend more fully *lectio divina*, and, unlike Vatican II's *Dei Verbum*, not only explicitly used the term but also quoted teaching about *lectio divina* derived from Origen, who had pioneered this method of biblical prayer (86–87).

On September 16, 2005, Pope Benedict used a brief address (to those participating in an international congress commemorating the fortieth anniversary of *Dei Verbum*) to "recall and recommend the ancient tradition of *lectio divina*." It had been proposed but not named as such in the closing chapter of the constitution (no. 25). Now forty years later the pope expressed his conviction that, "if effectively promoted, this practice will bring a new spiritual springtime to the Church."

Five years later Benedict XVI went beyond what his predecessor had briefly stated in *Ecclesia in America*. He explained that a prayerful reading of the Bible involved four steps: reading (*lectio*), meditation (*meditatio*), prayer (*oratio*), and contemplation (*contemplatio*) (*Verbum Domini* 87). While Benedict did not say so in *Verbum Domini*, this account of *lectio divina* was derived from Guigo II and John of the Cross.

In "Retrieving *Lectio Divina* at Vatican II and After," I describe more fully the post–Vatican II reception of *lectio divina* by popes and others (including Ernesto Cardenal and Carlo Maria Martini) and offer two examples of that practice.[21] Let me conclude by returning to the more schematic style of St. Ignatius, by providing a summary account of *lectio divina* and proffering a couple of examples.

- We can read the Scriptures with our prepared questions; we question the Scriptures on its use, for instance, of a verb (Mark 1:13; 1:31; 10:45; 15:41; *diakonein*, serve). Or we can let the Scriptures question us and speak to us.
- Read a passage slowly and three times; for transformation, not information; ruminate like a cow. Focus on words and phrases that stand out for you.
- Let associations float to the surface: for example, in Mark's use of *diakonein*.
- Let words ferment within you, like grape juice turning into wine. Let the word of God feed your heart:

---

for example, Alleluia (in the Hebrew Bible found only in the Psalms).

- "*Taste*, see, and experience that the Lord is sweet."
- The movements of the Holy Spirit. Where are we being taken by the Spirit?
- A deep sense of Presence; keep company with God. A brief gift or one that lasts? "Emmanuel, God with us" (Matt 1:23); "I will be with you always" (Matt 28:20).
- We are in God's arms like a child in her mother's arms (Ps 131:2). The way to read John's Gospel— leaning on the breast of Christ, enfolded by love.
- In *lectio divina* we start with God. If we start with ourselves, we will end with ourselves. If we gaze into ourselves, we will find only ourselves.

APPENDIX II

The Two Standards

[From Thomas G. Casey, *Wisdom at the Crossroads: The Life and Thought of Michael Paul Gallagher* (Mahwah, NJ: Paulist Press, 2018), 78–81; reproduced with permission.]

"The roots of this approach can be found in the spirituality of St Ignatius, which formed Michael Paul from his novitiate years. It is a spirituality that is highly hopeful and exceptionally realistic. It is hopeful, because Ignatius is convinced that God can be found in all things. It is realistic, because Ignatius sees life as a constant struggle between the powers of good and evil. Ignatius urges his followers to become aware of the inner struggle that is taking place all the time between authentic and counterfeit values, between truthfulness and falsehood. The major battle that goes on in our hearts takes place, not at the level of arguments and ideas, but at the affective level.

"In his decisive battle, Michael Paul was convinced that we must avoid becoming belligerent ourselves. Ironically we can only 'fight' this inner battle with the weapons of peace. The invitation, then, is for us to live out of the deeper level of ourselves, where we feel in tune with who we really are, for there it is that we find the grace to deal serenely not just with the struggles of our own hearts but with the struggles of our culture as well. If we drift through life on a superficial level, reacting instinctively rather than responding gracefully, then we will be trapped by our immature selves, and aggression will never be far away.

"One of the key meditations in the Spiritual Exercises, a meditation on the Two Standards, is designed to help us distinguish better between the destructive patterns that can seduce the heart and the call of Jesus to a radically different way. When Ignatius speaks of two standards, he is using imagery that would have been readily understood in the sixteenth century. He is referring to the two flags or military banners which were carried by opposing armies in battle. In the confusion of war, each soldier, by looking toward the raised flag or standard, instantly knew where his leader was in order to rally around him. The meditation called by this name is intended to enlighten our minds, so that in the midst of the complexities of our busy lives, we can recognize the person of Jesus and rally to his call. Michael Paul prayed on this exercise many times during the course of his life.

"In the meditation on the Two Standards, Ignatius presents us with formidable imagery. On the one hand, he asks us to imagine the gently appealing figure of Christ standing in the vicinity of Jerusalem. On the other hand, we are presented with the terrifying figure of Lucifer, seated on a throne of fire near Babylon. The sharp contrast between the two figures signifies how opposed they truly are. Their strategies for our world are also totally opposed. Jesus is shown gathering his followers around him and inviting them to go out and attract people to embrace his vision. In contrast, Satan aggressively 'summons innumerable demons' to him 'goading them' into laying snares for people. Then, having trapped them, they are to 'bind them with chains.' As Ignatius presents this meditation, he makes it clear that no place, no person, and no way of life is exempt from the competing claims of light and darkness. The battle is everywhere.

"This meditation is deeply rooted in Scripture, of course. 'No one can serve two masters,' says Jesus (Matt 12:30), and in the parable of the wheat and the weeds Jesus makes it clear that both good and evil are entangled together in this life (Matt 13:24–30). By opposing Jerusalem and Babylon, Ignatius is echoing the imagery of the Book of Revelation, which challenges us to choose either the peace, humility, and goodness of the New Jerusalem or the violent and arrogant opulence of Babylon. This vision of two opposing cities was later immortalized by St Augustine in his great work, *The City of God.* 'Two cities have been formed by two loves: the earthly by the love of self, even to the contempt of God; the heavenly by the love of God, even to the contempt of self.'

"Despite the grandiose military imagery that Ignatius uses, the meditation on the Two Standards is in fact about a battle that takes place primarily within our hearts. At this point in the Spiritual Exercises, the person making the retreat has already made a basic decision for Jesus. With this meditation, however, Ignatius wants to emphasize that the struggle is by no means over; it continues incessantly inside ourselves, at the level of our conflicting desires. We have to recommit ourselves to him again and again, because the battle is ongoing and we are always being drawn in contrary directions. We must repeatedly choose our standard and our leader.

"In Ignatius's paradigm, the 'enemy of our human nature' tempts us powerfully, and often subtly, by playing on our greed for possessions and for the prestige and adulation that often accompany them. Satan's ultimate goal is to bring us to 'overweening pride,' where God is effectively displaced by the self-absorbed individual. If this sounds like a summary of the message our consumerist society frequently transmits to us, it is surely a confirmation of the enduring relevance of Ignatius's insight.

"The standard of Jesus is radically different. Jesus invites us to see that everything is gift. It doesn't make sense to measure ourselves in terms of possessions or power, because nothing is truly ours. All we have points to the Giver, who is our loving Father and will continue to provide us with what we need. Instead of saying 'Look at me,' we are invited to say 'Look at God and all that God has done for me.' It is the message of the Beatitudes (Matt 5:1–12)."

NOTES

CHAPTER 1

1. C. G. Jung, *Psychological Reflections: A New Anthology of His Writings*, ed. J. Jacobi and R. F. C. Hull (London: Princeton University Press, 1971), 137–38.

2. See G. O'Collins, *The Second Journey: Spiritual Awareness and the Mid-Life Crisis*, 2nd ed. (Mahwah, NJ: Paulist Press, 1987).

3. What follows is told at greater length in the "Reminiscences" of Ignatius, translated and introduced with notes by Joseph Munitiz and Philip Endean, *Saint Ignatius of Loyola: Personal Writings* (London: Penguin 2004), 3–64.

4. Ludolph of Saxony, *Life of Jesus Christ*, trans. and intro. Milton Walsh, 4 vols. (Collegeville, MN: Liturgical Press, 2018–19).

5. For these quotations and a commentary on Ludolph's method, see M. Walsh, "'To Always Be Thinking Somehow about Jesus': The Prologue of Ludolph's *Vita Christi*," *Studies in the Spirituality of Jesuits* 43, no. 1 (Spring 2011): 10–12.

6. Munitiz and Endean, *Saint Ignatius of Loyola*, 29–38.

CHAPTER 2

1. The first person Dante meets in Paradise, Donati had joined a community of Franciscan nuns before she was forced to leave the convent and marry a rich and powerful man. According to one story, she died of a broken heart.

2. In canto one of the *Inferno*, Dante meets a leopard, a lion, and a she-wolf, which suggest three false paths in life (pleasure,

fame, and a desire for material possessions), and can be compared with John's "desire of the flesh, desire of the eyes, pride of life." One might name these three "drives" less negatively and speak of the desire to live, to possess, and to be somebody.

CHAPTER 3

1. Drawing on the Latin word (*colloquium*), Ignatius introduced the term *colloquy* to describe the familiar conversation (for example, with Jesus or the Blessed Virgin Mary) that he prescribes for the culmination of an exercise. But it may occur elsewhere—during an exercise. See SpEx 53–54, 61, 63, 71, 126, 199, 224, 225, 237; see also J. A. Munitiz and P. Endean, *Saint Ignatius of Loyola: Personal Writings*, new ed. (London: Penguin, 2004), xv.

2. The PF was included in the text of the Exercises submitted in 1548 for approval by Pope Paul III.

3. G. W. Hughes, *The God of Surprises* (Grand Rapids, MI: Eerdmans, 2008; orig. ed. 1991); Hughes, *God, Where Are You?* (London: Darton, Longman and Todd, 1997); R. Leonard, *Where the Hell Is God?* (Mahwah, NJ: Paulist Press, 2010).

4. Anthony de Mello cites Gandhi as endorsing a religious logic similar to the PF: "man's *ultimate aim* is the realization that all his activities have to be guided to the *ultimate aim* of the vision of God. The immediate service of all human beings becomes a necessary part of that endeavor, simply because the only way to find God is seeing him in his creation and to be one with him" (quoted, *Seek God Everywhere*, ed. G. O'Collins, D. Kendall, and J. LaBelle [New York: Doubleday, 2010], 11; italics mine).

5. R. Otto, *The Idea of the Holy*, trans. Melissa Raphael (Oxford: Clarendon Press,1997; German orig. 1917).

6. A. de Mello, *Seek God Everywhere: Reflections on the Spiritual Exercises of St. Ignatius*, ed. G. O'Collins, D. Kendall, and J. LaBelle (New York: Doubleday, 2010), 5.

7. de Mello, *Seek God Everywhere*, 9–11.

8. S. Arzubialde, *Ejercicios Espirituales de S. Ignacio: Historia y Análisis*, new ed. (Bilbao: Mensajero, 2009), 111–12. While holding that the final text of the PF had been elaborated by 1539, he notes a proposal that the elaboration continued even until 1544; Arzubialde, *Ejercicios Espirituales*, 112n5, 113.

9. In the *Canterbury Tales*, Geoffrey Chaucer describes the Wife of Bath as having taken five husbands to the door of a church to marry them (*Prologue*, 459–61).

10. M. Searle and K. W. Stevenson, *Documents of the Marriage Liturgy* (Collegeville, MN: Liturgical Press, 1992), 163.

11. Searle and Stevenson, *Documents of the Marriage Liturgy*, 166.

12. Searle and Stevenson, *Documents of the Marriage Liturgy*, 188–89.

13. C. Brooke, *The Medieval Idea of Marriage* (Oxford: Oxford University Press, 1989), 249. The major study used here by Brooke was P. Mutembe and J.-B. Molin, *Le Rituel du marriage en France du xiie au xvie siècle* (Paris: Beauchesne, 1974).

14. Brooke, *Medieval Idea of Marriage*, 251–52.

15. As stated above, I use the translation by Munitiz and Endean, *Saint Ignatius of Loyola: Personal Writings*, 289.

16. E. D. Hirsch, *Validity in Interpretation* (New Haven, CT: Yale University Press, 1967), 1.

17. P. Ricoeur, *Hermeneutics*, trans. D. Pellauer (Cambridge: Polity, 2013), 12.

18. P. Ricoeur, *Hermeneutics and the Human Sciences: Essays on Language, Action, Interpretation*, ed. and trans. J. B. Thompson (Cambridge: Cambridge University Press, 1981), 139.

19. Ricoeur, *Hermeneutics and the Human Sciences*, 211.

20. H.-G. Gadamer, *Truth and Method*, trans. J. Weinsheimer and D. G. Marshall, rev. ed. (New York: Crossroad, 1989), 296, 373, 395.

21. Arzubialde, *Ejercicios Spirituales*, 116, 117.

22. Arzubialde, *Ejercicios Spirituales*, 117n27.

23. Arzubialde, *Ejercicios Spirituales*, 118.

24. Arzubialde, *Ejercicios Spirituales*, 119.

25. Arzubialde, *Ejercicios Spirituales*, 122.

26. Arzubialde, *Ejercicios Spirituales*, 124.

CHAPTER 4

1. This translation from Dante follows Clive James, *The Divine Comedy* (New York: Liveright, 2013).

2. See "Angel," in *The Oxford Dictionary of the Christian Church*, 4th ed., ed. Andrew Louth (Oxford: Oxford University Press, 2022), 1:72–74.

3. S. Greenblatt, *The Rise and Fall of Adam and Eve* (London: Bodley Head, 2017).

4. I. Kant, *Critique of Pure Reason*, trans. P. Guyer and A. W. Wood (Cambridge: Cambridge University Press, 1998), 677.

5. M. P. Gallagher, *Dive Deeper: The Human Poetry of Faith* (London: Darton, Longman & Todd, 2002); see Thomas G. Casey, *Wisdom at the Crossroads: The Life and Thought of Michael Paul Gallagher, SJ* (Mahwah, NJ: Paulist Press, 2018).

6. For details, see Ralph Martin, *Will Many Be Saved? What Vatican II Actually Teaches and Its Implications for the New Evangelization* (Grand Rapids, MI: Eerdmans, 2012). See also G. O'Collins, "'Many Are Called but Few Are Chosen' (Matt 22:14). A Well-Populated Hell?" *Expository Times* 134 (2022): 64–70.

7. For a fuller treatment of this parable, see G. O'Collins, *Following the Way: Jesus as Our Spiritual Director* (London: HarperCollins, 1999), 165–72.

8. The classic New Testament episode in shifting the blame occurs in the passion story according to Matthew, when different characters try to shake off their responsibility for what is happening to Jesus. Judas brings the thirty pieces of silver back and tries to return the money to the chief priests and elders. "I have sinned," he says, "I have brought an innocent man to his death." But they won't accept the money from him. So he throws it down in the sanctuary and goes off to hang himself (Matt 27:3–5). Then the chief priests, in a way, try to shake off their responsibility. They take the money back, but do not put it into the temple fund. They use it to buy a field to serve as a burial place for foreigners (Matt 27:6–10). Pilate also tries to deny his responsibility for Jesus' fate by taking water and washing his hands in full view of the whole crowd (Matt 27:24).

9. In the case of the rich man and Lazarus, St. Gregory of Nyssa developed vividly the imagery of the drunken debauchery and celebrations of the rich man, his relatives, and his friends: *The Hungry are Dying: Beggars and Bishops in Roman Cappadocia*, trans. S. R. Holman (New York: Oxford University Press, 2001), 193–99.

10. St. Thomas Aquinas, *Summa Theologiae*, IIaIIae.27.1.

CHAPTER 5

1. "Reminiscences" (nr. 21), in J. A. Munitiz and P. Endean, *Saint Ignatius of Loyola: Personal Writings*, rev. ed. (London: Penguin, 2004), 22.

2. "Reminiscences," 22.

3. The *Exsultet* or Easter proclamation, sung on the vigil of Easter Sunday, goes back to the fifth century. It evokes key symbolic details of the original exodus from Egypt: "This is the night when first you saved our ancestors, you freed the people of Israel from their slavery and led them dry-shod through the sea. This is the night when the pillar of fire destroyed the darkness of sin." Imagery of victory over evil is also used by Venantius Fortunatus (d. around 619), Wipo of Burgundy (d. after 1046), and in the medieval celebration of Christ as the young Warrior who became the victorious Conqueror; see G. O'Collins, *Jesus our Redeemer* (Oxford: Oxford University Press, 2007), 116–32.

4. See the formula of the Institute of the Society of Jesus approved by Pope Paul III on September 27, 1540, through the apostolic letter *Regimini Militantis Ecclesiae*: "Whoever wishes to serve as a soldier of God beneath the banner of the cross in our society..." (1), *The Constitutions of the Society of Jesus and their Complementary Norms*, a complete English translation of the official Latin texts (St Louis: The Institute of Jesuit Sources, 1996), 3.

5. A. Vermeersch, *Miles Christi Jesu: Meditations on the Summary of the Constitutions* (Calcutta: Xavier Press, 1960; French orig., 1914).

6. The variety and numbers of people passing through the large railway station or major airport of a contemporary metropolis present a microcosm of all the human beings on the face of the earth.

7. Munitiz and Endean, *Saint Ignatius of Loyola: Personal Writings*, 25–26.

8. Trans. W. Lowrie, in *Parables of Kierkegaard*, ed. T. C. Oden (Princeton: Princeton University Press, 1978), 40–45.

CHAPTER 6

1. F. Bovon, *Luke: A Commentary*, 3 vols. (Minneapolis: Fortress Press, 2002–12) 1: 82; hereafter references to Bovon will be cited within my text.

2. Munitiz and Endean, eds., "Reminiscences," *Saint Ignatius of Loyola: Personal Writings*, 33–35.

3. Bovon allows that *phatnē* might mean here a "stable" or a "half-open feeding place, sometimes located in a cave." But he opts for "manger" and suggests that "the manger was probably made of stone (perhaps chiseled into the wall of a cave or the face of a rock) or of mud; wood was too expensive" (vol. 1, 90).

4. See Walter Bauer, Frederick W. Danker, William F. Arndt, and F. Wilbur Gingrich, eds., *Greek-English Lexicon of the New Testament and Other Early Christian Literature*, 3rd ed. (Chicago: University of Chicago Press, 2000), 1050; hereafter BDAG.

5. "An ox knows its owner, and a donkey its master's stall" (Isa 1:3; Revised English Bible).

6. BDAG, 1050.

7. Joseph A. Fitzmyer, *The Gospel According to Luke I–IX* (New York: Doubleday, 1981), 408.

8. Roman A. Siebenrock, "Jesus Christ: Life as Passion for the Kingdom of God," in *"Godhead Here in Hiding": Incarnation and the History of Human Suffering*, ed. Terrence Merrigan and Frederik Glorieux (Leuven: Peeters, 2012), 37.

9. I have not found any commentator on the Spiritual Exercises who remarks on the way, apropos of Christ's nativity, Ignatius's notes for the mysteries of Christ's life differ partially from what has been stated in the contemplation on the nativity in SpEx 110–17.

10. At least as old as the eighth-century BCE epic poet Homer, *inclusio* is a technique for linking the beginning and end of some short or long piece of writing. We detect an *inclusio* by noting the similar or even identical material found at the beginning and the end of the work or section in question.

11. Bovon (vol. 3, 144–45) argues convincingly against introducing hard "furniture" such as couches; what Luke has in mind are soft objects, for example, carpets or even blankets.

12. BDAG, 521.

13. BDAG, 753.

14. Raymond Brown joins others in questioning "the image of the hard-hearted innkeeper turning Joseph and Mary away from the door. Rather, all that Luke is saying is that, because travelers were sheltered in one crowded room," the inn was not a fitting place for the birth. The innkeeper was "correct rather than hard-hearted. He refused accommodation to (the obviously pregnant) Mary because if she went into labor and gave birth in the place where people were lodged, the other guests would have been inconvenienced by having to go out from it." Nevertheless, Brown shows himself at least open to the notion of "rejection." It fits "the larger Lucan picture," by anticipating "the career of the Son of Man who will be rejected" (*The Birth of the Messiah: A Commentary on the Infancy Narratives in the Gospels of Matthew and Luke*, rev. ed. [New York: Doubleday, 1993], 670).

15. Bovon, vol. 2, 56, fn24. Bovon lists here "example stories" that Luke has drawn from L, his special sources: for example, the rich farmer (12:16–21), the rich man and the poor Lazarus (16:19–31), and the Pharisee and the tax collector (18:10–14).

16. Martin Luther identified Christ as the Good Samaritan and made the inn a kind of field hospital (Erwin Mülhaupt, *D. Martin Luthers Evangelien-Auslegung*, vol. 3 [Göttingen: Vandenhoeck & Ruprecht, 1968], 152–56).

17. Here Peter and John act as servants; after the resurrection and Pentecost they will be twinned as the Church's first leaders; on Peter and John leading together, see Acts 3:1, 11; 4:3, 19; and 8:14.

18. St. Bonaventure, as cited by Bovon (vol. 3, 146).

19. On this see more fully G. O'Collins, *Salvation for All: God's Other Peoples* (Oxford: Oxford University Press, 2008), 100–20.

CHAPTER 7

1. Pope Francis's apostolic exhortation *Gaudete et Exsultate*, On the Call to Holiness in Today's World, of March 19, 2018 (Vatican City: Libreria Editrice Vaticana, 2018), relates repeatedly to issues raised by the meditation on the Two Standards. More generally, we can understand this exhortation as a contemporary rereading of the Spiritual Exercises, even if it does not present itself as such. A brilliant account of the Two Standards has come from Thomas G. Casey, *Wisdom at the Crossroads: The Life and Thought of Michael Paul Gallagher*

(Mahwah, NJ: Paulist Press, 2018). With permission, Casey's account is reproduced in an appendix to this book.

2. According to John 15:15, Christ says, "I no longer call you servants [*doulous*]. I have called you friends [*philous*]." According to the philosophy of language and speech-acts theory developed by John L. Austin (1911–60), performative utterances not only describe a given reality but also change what they describe. By calling us friends, Christ also makes us his friends.

3. See a 1534 letter of Ignatius to Isabel Roser in J.M. Munitiz and P. Endean, eds., *Saint Ignatius of Loyola: Personal Writings*, 2nd ed. (London: Penguin, 2004), 126.

4. Trans. John Drury (New York: Paulist Press, 1968).

5. Metz, *Poverty of Spirit*, 25–26; trans. corrected.

6. G. O'Collins, *The Beauty of Jesus Christ* (Oxford: Oxford University Press, 2020). The question opens up for Christian believers: Where do I find a satisfying image of the beautiful Jesus? In the work of Warner Sallman (d. 1968), whose 50 million pictures made him the most reproduced artist of twentieth-century America? In Eastern icons, or in the works of Caravaggio, Chagall, Dali, El Greco, Hunt, Piero della Francesca, Rembrandt, Rouault, and other artists, ancient and modern, from the five continents of the world?

7. On the Three Classes and the need to be interiorly free, see A. de Mello, *Seek God Everywhere*, 78–83.

8. D. E. Nineham, *Saint Mark* (London: Penguin, 1992; orig. 1963), 80–81.

9. Significantly, it is in relation to Peter that a young *paidiskē* of the high priest is brought into the story at the end, just as an older, also anonymous, woman enters the story as Peter's mother-in-law at the beginning.

10. Is she a widow? There is no reference to her husband, Peter's father-in-law. She lives in a house owned by the two brothers, Simon Peter and Andrew; there is no reference to their parents (dead or living elsewhere?). Peter's mother-in-law seems to run the household and would be expected to show hospitality to any guests. The silence about Peter's wife has led some to imagine that at this point he was a widower and only remarried later (see 1 Cor 9:5).

11. S. Miller, *Women in Mark's Gospel* (London: T. & T. Clark, 2004), 2.

12. M. Eugene Boring notes that "now restored to the fullness of life," she "can serve guests in her own home, which she had been prevented from doing by the devastating fever" (*Mark: A Commentary* [Louisville, KY: Westminster John Knox, 2006], 66). This observation stops short of noting how she is the only person cured by Jesus in Mark's Gospel who then does something for him (and his disciples). As Miller writes, "it is the only narrative in which a human being responds to Jesus' healing with service" (*Women in Mark's Gospel*, 22; see also 30). Bartimaeus is an exception here; after his healing, he does something for Jesus by "following" him "on the road" to the crucifixion and resurrection (Mark 10:52). He differs, of course, from Peter's mother-in-law in that it is he who informs Jesus of his situation (blindness) and asks for healing.

13. Miller, *Women in Mark's Gospel*, 29.

14. Mary Ann Tolbert comments: "the author of Mark, by using the same word for the action of angels and the action of the healed woman, obviously equated their level of service to Jesus" ("Mark," in Carol A. Newsom and Sharon H. Ringe, eds., *The Women's Bible Commentary* [Louisville, KY: Westminster John Knox Press, 1992], 263–74, at 267). Tolbert also observes how Peter's mother-in-law is "the first women to appear in the Gospel of Mark" ("Mark," 267), but fails to note how she is the only person cured by Jesus in that Gospel who then does something for him.

15. To relate the use of *serve* in various contexts does not entail assigning it a monolithic meaning but rather noting similar, overlapping meanings.

16. J. R. Donahue and D. J. Harrington, *The Gospel of Mark* (Collegeville, MN: Liturgical Press, 2002), 85.

17. M. E. Boring, *Mark: A Commentary* (Louisville, KY: Westminster John Knox, 2006), 66.

18. Nineham, *Saint Mark*, 81.

19. C. Focant, *The Gospel According to Mark*, trans. Leslie Robert Keylock (Eugene, OR: Pickwick Publications, 2012), 72.

20. The word order in Nineham's translation also parallels a general rule in Greek: "the aorist participle is normally, though by no means always, *antecedent* in time to the action of the main verb" (Daniel B. Wallace, *Greek Grammar beyond the Basics: An Exegetical Syntax of the New Testament* [Grand Rapids, MI: Zondervan, 1996], 624; italics original).

21. Wallace, *Greek Grammar*, 71, 72.

22. Foçant notes more accurately that "there is no explicit request for healing, contrary to the usual practice in the miracle narratives. There is at the very most a secret hope, an indirect request that is translated by speaking to Jesus about the ill person" (*Gospel According to Mark*, 72). Boring even thinks that the disciples "tell Jesus of her malady more likely to excuse her conduct than as a request for healing—Jesus has as yet performed no healings in Mark" (*Mark*, 66).

23. F. J. Moloney, *The Gospel of Mark: A Commentary* (Peabody, MA: Hendrickson, 2002), 55.

24. Moloney, *The Gospel of Mark*, 55.

25. M. D. Hooker, *The Gospel According to Mark* (London: Continuum, 2001), 70.

26. At least as old as the eighth-century BC epic poet, Homer, *inclusio* is a technique for linking (for various purposes) the beginning and the end of a poem, historical work, drama, prayer, biography, or some other written work—not to mention its role in spoken performances. *Inclusio* may be used for an entire work or simply for a section of a work. We detect the presence of *inclusio* by observing the similar or even identical material found at the beginning and the end of the work or section in question.

27. Moloney, *Gospel of Mark*, 56n46.

28. Hooker, *Gospel According to Mark*, 70.

29. J. Marcus, *Mark 1–8* (New York: Doubleday, 2000), 199. Hence, while contexts differ, the "raising" of Peter's mother-in-law and the "raising" of Jesus justify associating Mark 1:41 and 16:6 and using this association as *part* of the argument for recognizing an *inclusio* (see later).

30. Marcus, *Mark 1–8*, 199.

31. Marcus, *Mark 1–8*, 73–75.

32. In other places Paul uses *diakonein* and related forms to speak of the new life of the baptized as a life of service (for example, 2 Cor 3:3; 6:4; 11:8; and 11:23).

33. D. Krause, "Simon Peter's Mother-in-Law—Disciple or Domestic Servant," in *A Feminist Companion to Mark*, ed. Amy-Jill Levine (Sheffield: Sheffield Academic Press, 2001), 37–53, at 39.

Krause fails to note either that Peter's mother-in-law is the first woman mentioned in Mark's Gospel or that she is (possibly except for Bartimaeus) the only person in that gospel who is cured by Jesus and then does something for him.

34. Krause, "Simon Peter's Mother-in-Law," 50. Peter-Ben Smit has taken issue with Krause's article: performing household tasks does not exhaust the meaning of *diakonein* in Mark 1:29–31. He finds "a very special feature of the healing" in the fact that "the story is the only one in which the healing of an ill person is followed by [a] concrete and positive response towards Jesus" ("Simon Peter's Mother-in-Law Revisited," *Lectio difficilior* 1 (2003): 1–12. But Smit sees nothing special in the fact that Peter's mother-in-law is the first woman to be mentioned in Mark's Gospel.

35. See E. Schüssler Fiorenza, *In Memory of Her: A Feminist Reconstruction of Christian Origins*, rev. ed. (London: SCM Press, 1994), 320–21.

36. Other commentators on Mark's Gospel (James R. Edwards, R. T. France, Joachim Gnilka, Rudolf Pesch, Eduard Schweizer, Robert H. Stein, Mark L. Strauss, and Vincent Taylor) also fail to refer to her being the first woman named in the Gospel. They do not raise the possibility of her featuring in a significant *inclusio* between the opening and conclusion of that Gospel.

37. Adela Yarbro Collins, *Mark: A Commentary* (Minneapolis: Fortress Press, 2007), 174–75.

38. Apropos of Mark 1:31 and 15:41, Miller remarks that "Jesus' mission is framed by two references to the service of women" (*Women in Mark's Gospel*, 23), and that "the conclusion of the Gospel draws Mark's audience back to the beginning" (199). But she does not speak explicitly of an "*inclusio*."

39. R. Bauckham, *Jesus and the Eyewitnesses: The Gospels as Eyewitness Testimony* (Grand Rapids, MI: Eerdmans, 2006), 155–81.

40. Apropos of Mark 15:41, Adela Yarbro Collins comments, "The only woman that Mark portrays earlier in the narrative as serving Jesus is the mother-in-law of Simon (1:31)" (*Mark*, 774–75). This comment ignores the anonymous woman of Mark 14:3–9, who does something remarkable for Jesus even if her action is not called service and takes place in Bethany (near Jerusalem), not in Galilee.

CHAPTER 8

1. *Gaudium et Spes*, in Austin Flannery, *Vatican Council II: The Conciliar and Post Conciliar Documents*, rev. ed. (Northport, NY: Costello Publishing, 1988), 937.

2. In G. O'Collins, D. Kendall and J. LaBelle, eds., *Seek God Everywhere: Reflections on the Spiritual Exercises of St. Ignatius* (New York: Doubleday, 2010), 139–46; on the elections see 84–99.

CHAPTER 9

1. See Brian O'Leary, "Third and Fourth Weeks: What the Directories Say," *The Way* Supplement 58 (Spring 1987): 3–20.

2. G. O'Collins, *Reflections for Busy People: Making Time for Ourselves, Jesus, and God* (Mahwah, NJ: Paulist Press, 2009), 84–86.

3. Two vols. (New York: Doubleday, 1994).

4. On the way to Calvary, the Roman soldiers forced a passerby, Simon of Cyrene, to carry the cross for Jesus, who was very weakened by a savage scourging (15:21). By naming Simon of Cyrene and his two sons, Alexander and Rufus, Mark suggests that they were known to the Christian community. Did the service Simon was compelled to accept so affect him that he became a disciple of Jesus and so did his family?

5. See G. O'Collins, *The Beauty of Jesus Christ* (Oxford: Oxford University Press, 2020), 106–10.

6. O'Collins, *Beauty of Jesus Christ*, 110–16.

CHAPTER 10

1. Trans. John Shea (London: Burns & Oates, 1964), 79–86, at 86.

2. Bruce M. Metzger, *A Textual Commentary on the Greek New Testament*, 2nd ed. (Stuttgart: United Bible Societies, 1994), 151.

3. F. Bovon, *Luke*, vol. 3, trans. James Crouch (Minneapolis: Fortress Press, 2012), 211. Bovon discusses in depth Luke 22:43–44 (195–99, 201–11) and lists those who join him in favoring Lukan authenticity (199, n37). To this list we can add Raymond E. Brown, *The Death of the Messiah*, vol. 1 (New York: Doubleday, 1994), 179–90.

4. G. O'Collins, *The Beauty of Jesus Christ* (Oxford: Oxford University Press, 2020).

5. Gabriele Finaldi et al., eds., *The Image of Christ: The Catalogue of the Exhibition* (London: National Gallery, 2000).

6. Finaldi, *Image of Christ*, 105–31.

7. Finaldi, *Image of Christ*, 132–67.

8. Many editions of Pascal's *Pensées* list this as number 552—for example, W. F. Trotter's translation (New York: E. P. Dutton, 1958). It is *Pensée* 616 in A. J. Krailsheimer's translation (London: Penguin, 1966) that adopts the order of the *Pensées* as Pascal left them at his death.

9. In Helen Gardner, ed., *The Faber Book of Religious Verse* (London: Faber & Faber, 1972), 30.

CHAPTER 11

1. Helen Gardner provides the relevant sections from Langland's visionary poem in *The Faber Book of Religious Verse* (London: Faber & Faber. 1972), 39–48.

2. G. O'Collins, "Christ's Descent to the Dead: A Commentary," *Worship* 96 (2022): 178–85.

3. See J. D. Breckenridge, "Et prima vidit: The Iconography of the Appearance of Christ to His Mother," *Art Bulletin* 39 (1957): 9–32; Peter-Hans Kolvenbach, *La Pasqua di nostra Signora* (Rome: Centrum Ignatianum Spiritualitatis, 1988); Jack Mahoney, "The Risen Jesus and His Mother," *Thinking Faith*, December 29, 2011; C. Vona, "L'apparizione di Gesù risorto alla madre sua negli antichi scritti Cristiani," *Divinitas* 1 (1957): 479–527. I draw on these authors for what has been said about the appearance to Mary.

4. *Saint Ignatius of Loyola: Personal Writings*, trans. J. A. Munitiz and P. Endean, 2nd ed. (London: Penguin, 2004), 132–33.

5. See Centrum Ignatianum Spiritualitatis, *The Trinity in the Ignatian Charism*, CIS, vol. 13 (Rome: CIS, 1982); G. O'Collins, "Pentecost Then and Now," *Pastoral Review* 18 (2022): 59–62.

6. See G. O'Collins, "Jesus and Mary," *The Furrow* 73 (2022): 162–64.

CHAPTER 12

1. See Michael J. Buckley, "The Contemplation to Attain Love," in *The Way Supplement* 24 (Spring 1975): 92–104.

2. See G. O'Collins, "Love as a Verb (1 Cor 13:4–8a)," in *Illuminating the New Testament: The Gospels, Acts, and Paul* (Mahwah, NJ: Paulist Press, 2022), 159–64.

3. On this interior knowledge, see chapter 2 above, under "the General Examen of Conscience and Consciousness."

4. On the Contemplation for Attaining Love, see Santiago Arzubialde, *Ejercicios Espirituales de S. Ignacio: Historia y Análisis*, new ed. (Bilbao: Mensajero, 2009), 557–82. On the three powers of the soul, especially memory, see G. O'Collins, "Memory, *The Spiritual Exercises* and John 21," *The Way* 49 (2020): 67–76.

5. The following paragraph invokes repeatedly the second power of the soul: "to see," "the gift of understanding," "understand," and "reflect within myself."

6. On John as such a source, see O'Collins, "Memory, *The Spiritual Exercises* and John 21," 67–76.

7. The evangelist remarks that the appearance of Jesus by the Sea of Tiberias was "the third time that Jesus was manifested to the disciples after he was raised from the dead" (John 21:14). Yes, it was the third time that Jesus appeared to a *group* of disciples, but not the third time absolutely: he did appear first to Mary Magdalene (John 20:11–18).

8. See David Coffey, "The Ignatian *Suscipe* Prayer: Its Text and Meaning," *Journal of Jesuit Studies* 5 (2018): 511–29. Attached to the first point proposed by Ignatius, this prayer asks that I receive the grace to love (more and more) God. It concerns my love for God. But points 2, 3, and 4 concern the ways God shows love for me and, indeed, for all created realities. This love is simply there, like the divine mercy, which exercitants do not need to ask for directly. They have only to open their minds and hearts to it (see chapter 4 above).

9. For love leading to truth, see G. O'Collins, *The Beauty of Jesus Christ* (Oxford: Oxford University Press, 2020), 10–13.

APPENDIX I

1. *The New Testament with Lectio Divina* (Mahwah, NJ: Paulist Press, 2020). See Raymond Studzinski, *Reading to Live: The Evolving Practice of* Lectio Divina (Collegeville, MN: Liturgical Press, 2009).

2. Theonas of Alexandria, *Letter to Lucianus*, 9, *Anti-Nicene Christian Library*, vol. 6 (Edinburgh: T. & T. Clark, 1869), 160–61.

3. *Epistola ad Gregorium*, no. 3, in *Anti-Nicene Christian Library*, vol. 10, *The Writings of Origen* (Edinburgh: T. & T. Clark, 1869), 390.

4. See Jacques Rousse et al., "*Lectio divina* et lecture spirituelle," in *Dictionnaire de Spiritualité*, vol. 9 (Paris: Beauchesne, 1978), cols. 476–510. For an introduction to the immense literature on Origen, see "Origen," in *The Oxford Dictionary of the Christian Church*, ed. Andrew Louth (Oxford: Oxford University Press, 2022): II:1405–6.

5. The Pontifical Biblical Commission, *The Interpretation of the Bible in the Church* (Vatican City: Libreria Editrice Vaticana, 1993), 121–22.

6. Timothy Fry, ed., *The Rule of St. Benedict in Latin and English* (Collegeville, MN: Liturgical Press, 1981), 249–53; see also 95–96, 446–47, 467–68.

7. Guigo II, *The Ladder of Monks. A Letter on the Contemplative Life and Twelve Meditations*, trans. Edmund College and James Walsh (Kalamazoo, MI: Cistercian Publications, 1978), 17–20, 69–74.

8. See Pascale Dominique Nau, *When God Speaks:* Lectio Divina *in Saint John of the Cross, The Ladder of Monks and the Rule of Carmel* (San Sebastian: Villa Alaidi, 2012).

9. For Leclercq on *lectio divina*, see *The Love of Learning and the Desire for God*, trans. Catherine Misrahi (New York: Fordham University Press, 1982; French orig. 1957). Leclercq "showed how monastic theology grew out of the practice of *lectio divina*" (Studzinski, *Reading to Live*, 192).

10. I translate directly from the original (Latin) text of *Dei Verbum*, found in *Sacrosanctum Oecumenicum Concilium Vaticanum II, Constitutiones Decreta Declarationes* (Vatican City: Typis Polyglottis Vaticanis, 1966).

11. St. Augustine, *Sermo* 179, *Sermons* (148–83), trans. Edmund Hill (New Rochelle, NY: New City Press, 1992), 298.

12. Jerome, *Commentarium in Isaiam*, prologue, *Patrologia Latina* (PL), vol. 24, col. 178.

13. J. Wicks, "Scripture Reading Urged Vehementer (DV No. 25): Background and Development," *Theological Studies* 74 (2013): 555–80.

14. The Decree on the Training of Priests (*Optatam Totius*), promulgated on October 28, 1965, alluded to *lectio divina* when

it mandated that seminarians should be "taught to seek Christ in faithful meditation on the word of God" (8). The Decree on Ecumenism (*Unitatis Redintegratio*), promulgated on November 21, 1964, gave a trinitarian account of what other Christians do in what can be rightly called their practice of *lectio divina*: "While invoking the Holy Spirit, in these very Sacred Scriptures they search out God speaking to them in Christ" (21). Thus we can name four decrees of Vatican II that retrieve and encourage *lectio divina*.

15. The Flannery translation is misleading when it renders "*lectione divina*" as "spiritual reading": Austin Flannery, ed., *Vatican Council II: The Conciliar and Post Conciliar Documents* (Northport, NY: Costello Publishing, rev. ed., 1987), 896. While *lectio divina*, both traditionally and in the teaching of Vatican II, involves prayerfully meditating on biblical texts, spiritual reading does not as such involve meditation and can be engaged with such nonscriptural works as *Introduction to the Devout Life* by St. Francis de Sales or the writings of St. Thérèse of Lisieux.

16. Wicks, "Scripture Reading," 571.

17. Norman P. Tanner, ed., *Decrees of the Ecumenical Councils*, vol. 2 (Washington, DC: Georgetown University Press, 1990), 1065.

18. Marianne Lorraine Trouvé, ed., *The Sixteen Documents of Vatican II* (Boston: Pauline Books & Media, 1999), 607. Spiritual reading does not as such involve meditation and, as we have already seen, can be engaged with nonscriptural texts such as *Introduction to the Devout Life* by St. Francis de Sales.

19. *The Interpretation of the Bible in the Church*, 121–22.

20. *Catechism of the Catholic Church* (Homebush, NSW: St Paul's, 1994), no. 1177; see no. 2708.

21. G. O'Collins, "Retrieving *Lectio Divina* at Vatican II and After," *The Way* 60 (2021): 87–100.

BIBLIOGRAPHY

I

Arzubialde, Santiago. *Ejercicios Espirituales de S. Ignacio: Historia y Análisis*, new ed. Bilbao: Mensajero, 2009.

Aschenbrenner, George A. *Stretched for Greater Glory: What to Expect from the Spiritual Exercises*. Chicago: Loyola, 2004.

Barry, William A. *Allowing the Creator to Deal with the Creature: An Approach to the Spiritual Exercises of Ignatius of Loyola*. Mahwah, NJ: Paulist Press, 1994.

Cusson, Gilles. *Biblical Theology and the Spiritual Exercises: A Method toward a Personal Experience of God as Accomplishing within Us His Plan of Salvation*. St. Louis: Institute of Jesuit Sources, 1998.

Endean, Philip. "Spiritual Exercises." In *The Cambridge Encyclopedia of the Jesuits*, edited by Thomas Worcester, 757–62. Cambridge: Cambridge University Press, 2017.

Fleming, David K. *Draw Me into Your Friendship: A Literal Translation and Contemporary Reading of the Spiritual Exercises*. St. Louis: Institute of Jesuit Sources, 1996.

———— ed., *Notes on the Spiritual Exercises of St. Ignatius of Loyola*. St. Louis: Review for Religious, 1981.

Futrell, John C., and Marian Cowan. *Companions in Grace: A Handbook for Directors of the Spiritual Exercises of Saint Ignatius of Loyola*. St. Louis: Institute of Jesuit Sources, 2000.

Gallagher, Timothy M. *The Discernment of Spirits: An Ignatian Guide for Everyday Living*. New York: Crossroad, 2005.

————. *The Examen Prayer: Ignatian Wisdom for Our Lives Today*. New York: Crossroad, 2006.

————. *Spiritual Consolation: An Ignatian Guide for the Greater Discernment of Spirits.* New York: Crossroad, 2007.

Goulding, Gill K. *A Church of Passion and Hope.* London: Bloomsbury, 2015; on the eighteen rules for thinking, judging, and feeling with the Church (SpEx 353–70).

Green, Thomas H. *Weeds among the Wheat: Discernment; Where Prayer and Action Meet.* Notre Dame, IN: Ave Maria Press, 1990.

Hansen, Michael. *The First Exercises.* Notre Dame, IN: Ave Maria Press, 2013.

Iparraguirre, Ignacio. *Historia de la prática de los Ejercicios Espirituales de San Ignacio de Loyola,* 3 vols. Bilbao: El Mensajero del Corajón de Jesus, 1946–73.

Ivens, Michael. *Understanding the Spiritual Exercises.* Leominster, Herefordshire: Gracewing, 1998.

Liebert, Elizabeth, and Annemarie Paulin-Campbell. *The Spiritual Exercises Reclaimed: Uncovering Liberating Possibilities for Women,* 2nd ed. Mahwah, NJ: Paulist Press, 2022.

Martin, James J. *Together on Retreat: Meeting Jesus in Prayer.* New York: HarperOne, 2013.

Munitiz, Joseph A., and Philip Endean. *Saint Ignatius of Loyola: Personal Writings.* London: Penguin, 1996.

O'Collins, Gerald. "Marriage Vows and the Principle and Foundation," *The Way* 58 (2019): 19–24.

————. "Memory in the Spiritual Exercises and John 21," *The Way* 59 (2020): 67–76.

————. "Retrieving *Lectio Divina* at Vatican II and After." *The Way* 60 (2021): 87–100.

O'Collins, Gerald, Daniel Kendall, and Jeffrey LaBelle, eds., *Seek God Everywhere: Reflections on the Spiritual Exercises of St. Ignatius* (by Anthony de Mello). New York: Doubleday, 2010.

O'Reilly, Terence. *The Spiritual Exercises of Saint Ignatius of Loyola: Contexts, Sources, Reception.* Leiden: Brill, 2020.

Schemel, George J., and Judith A. Roemer. *Beyond Individuation to Discipleship: A Directory for Those Who Give the Spiritual Exercises.* Scranton, PA: Institute for Contemporary Spirituality, 2000.

Sheldrake, Philip, ed. *The Way of Ignatius Loyola: Contemporary Approaches to the Spiritual Exercises.* St. Louis: Institute of Jesuit Sources, 1991.

Tellechea Idígoras, José Ignacio. *Ignatius of Loyola: The Pilgrim Saint*, trans. Cornelius Michael Buckley. Chicago: Loyola University Press, 1994.

Tetlow, Joseph A. *Always Discerning*. Chicago: Loyola Press, 2016.

———. *Choosing Christ in the World: Directing the Spiritual Exercises of St. Ignatius Loyola*. St. Louis: Institute of Jesuit Sources, 2000.

Tetlow, Joseph A., and Carol Atwell Ackeis. *Finding Christ in the World: A Twelve-week Ignatian Retreat*. St. Louis: Institute of Jesuit Sources, 2013.

Toner, Jules J. *A Commentary on Saint Ignatius' Rules for the Discernment of Spirits: A Guide to the Principles and Practice*. St. Louis: Institute of Jesuit Sources, 1982.

———. *Discerning God's Will*. St. Louis: Institute of Jesuit Sources, 1991.

———. *Ignatius Loyola: Spiritual Exercises*. New York: Crossroad, 1992.

Williams, Monty. *The Gift of Spiritual Intimacy: Following the Spiritual Exercises of Saint Ignatius*. Toronto: Novalis, 2009.

Supplements to *The Way* (1965 to 2002) have been dedicated to themes of *The Spiritual Exercises*: for instance, 18 (Spring 1973) on "the Kingdom"; 48 (Autumn 1983) on "Presenting the First Week"; 49 (Spring 1984) on "The Spiritual Exercises in Daily Life"; 55 (Spring 1986) on "From Loyola to La Mancha" (three articles on "The Two Standards"); 58 (Spring 1987) on "The Spiritual Exercises: Weeks Three and Four"; supplement 2000/99, on "Resurrection and Beyond."

II. GERALD O'COLLINS: BOOKS RELEVANT TO THE *SPIRITUAL EXERCISES*

The Calvary Christ. London: SCM Press, 1977.

A Month with Jesus. Denville, NJ: Dimension Books, 1978; the diary of a thirty-day retreat.

Finding Jesus: Living Through Lent with John's Gospel. New York: Paulist Press, 1983.

The People's Christmas. New York: Paulist Press, 1984.

Experiencing Jesus. London: SPCK, 1994.

All Things New. Mahwah, NJ: Paulist Press, 1998.

Following the Way: Jesus Our Spiritual Director. London: Harper Collins, 1999.

The Lord's Prayer. London: Darton, Longman & Todd, 2006.

Jesus: A Portrait. London: Darton, Longman & Todd, 2008.

Reflections for Busy People: Making Time for Ourselves, Jesus, and God. Mahwah, NJ: Paulist Press, 2009.

Pause for Thought: Making Time for Prayer, Jesus, and God. Mahwah, NJ: Paulist Press, 2011.

The Spirituality of the Second Vatican Council. Mahwah, NJ: Paulist Press, 2014.

Letters to Nevie: Learning from the Scriptures. London: St. Paul's Publishing, 2016.

Saint Augustine on the Resurrection of Christ. Oxford: Oxford University Press, 2017.

Moments of Grace. Buxhall, Stowmarket, Suffolk: Kevin Mayhew, 2018.

The Beauty of Jesus Christ. Oxford: Oxford University Press, 2020.

Illuminating the New Testament: The Gospels, Acts, and Paul. Mahwah, NJ: Paulist Press, 2022.

INDEX OF NAMES

Abbado, Claudio, 94

Abel, 47

Abraham, F. Murray, 56

Abraham the patriarch, 2, 12, 28

Ackeis, Carol Atwell, 177

Adam, 39, 47, 93, 125, 126, 162

Aeneas, 5

Alacoque, St. Margaret Mary, 113–14

Alighieri, Dante, 2, 4–5, 11–12, 37, 43, 159, 161

Ambrose of Milan, St., 127, 146–48

Aquinas, St. Thomas, 39, 41, 162

Arndt, William F., 164

Arzubialde, Santiago, 30, 34–35, 160–61, 170, 175

Aschenbrenner, George, 17, 175

Augustine of Hippo, St., 20, 44, 135, 144, 146–48, 156–57, 173

Augustus, Emperor, 64, 65

Austin, John L., 166

Bach, Johann Sebastian, 45, 115, 116, 125

Balthasar, Hans Urs von, 45

Barry, William A., 175

Bauckham, Richard, 90, 169

Bauer, Walter, 164

Beethoven, Ludwig van, 94

Bellow, Saul, 95

Benedict of Nursia, St., 145, 147, 173

Benedict XVI, Pope, 136, 145, 151–52

Berlin, Irving, 144

Bernanos, Georges, 22

Blessed Virgin Mary, *passim*

Bonaventure, St., 165

Bonhoeffer, Dietrich, 2–5

Boring, M. Eugene, 85, 167–68

Bosch, Hieronymus, 41

Botticelli, Sandro, 67, 68

Bovon, François x, 64, 68–70, 72–76, 114, 164–65, 170

Braybrooke, Neville, 119–21

Breckenridge, James D., 171

Britten, Benjamin, 115

Brooke, Christopher, 31–32, 161

Brown, Raymond E., 108, 165, 170

Buckley, Cornelius Michael, 177

Buckley, Michael J., 171

Bunyan, John, 2

Byrne, Brendan, ix, x

Cadwallader, Alan ix
Cain, 47–48
Caravaggio, 92–93, 166
Cardenal, Ernesto, 145, 152
Carter, Jimmy, 2, 4
Casey, Thomas G., ix, 155–57,
    162, 165–66
Catalina, Princess, 6, 7
Chagall, Marc, 166
Chaplain, Charlie, 10
Charles V, Emperor, 1, 6
Chaucer, Geoffrey, 161
Christ, *passim*
Coffey, David, 172
College, Edmund, 173
Collins, Adela Yarbro,
    90, 169
Cook, Sarah, ix
Cowan, Marian, 175
Crilly, Donna, ix
Crossman, Samuel, 116
Crouch, James, 170
Curtin, Steve, ix
Cusson, Giles, 175

Dalí, Salvador, 166
Danker, Frederick W., 164
David, King, 48
Deak, Alicia, ix
De Mello, Anthony, viii, 30, 35,
    101, 160, 166, 176
Denver, John, 62
Dodd, Liz, 49
Dominic, St., 6
Donahue, John R., 85, 167
Donati, Piccarda, 11, 159
Drury, John, 166
Duns Scotus, 39
Dürer, Albrecht, 126

Edwards, James R., 169
El Greco, 166
Elijah, 94–96
Eliot, T. S., 2, 5
Endean, Philip, viii, ix, 159–61,
    163–64, 166, 171, 175–76
Ephrem, St., 127
Epiphanius of Salamis, 126
Erasmus of Rotterdam, 30
Eve, 39, 47, 125
Evely, George, 30

Finaldi, Gabriele, 171
Fiorenza, Elisabeth Schüssler,
    89, 169
Fitzmyer, Joseph A., 164
Flannery, Austin, 151, 170, 174
Fleming, David K., 175
Foçant, Camille, 85–86, 88,
    167–68
France, Richard T., 169
Francis, Pope, 6, 143, 165
Francis de Sales, St., 174
Francis of Assisi, St., 6, 66
Frank, César, 115
Fry, Timothy, 173
Futrell, John C., 175

Gadamer, Hans-Georg, 34, 161
Gallagher, Michael Paul, 42,
    155–56, 162, 165
Gallagher, Timothy M., 175–76
Gandhi, Mahatma, 27, 160
Gardner, Helen, 171
Gascoyne, David, 79, 117
Geertgen Tot Sint Jans, 67
George of Nicodemia, St., 127
Gerhardt, Paul, 116
Gertrude of Helfta, St., 113

Gingrich, F. Wilbur, 164
Glorieux, Frederik, 164
Glynn, Patrick McMahon, 38
Gnilka, Joachim, 169
Goulding, Gill K., 176
Gounod, Charles, 115
Green, Thomas H., 176
Greenblatt, Stephen, 39, 162
Gregory of Neocaesarea,
    St., 146
Gregory of Nyssa, St., 162
Grünewald, Matthias, 67, 106
Guigo II, 147, 152, 178
Guyer, Paul D., 162

Hansen, Michael, 176
Harrington, Daniel J., 85, 167
Haydn, Franz Josef, 115
Hemingway, Ernest, 15
Herod Antipas, King, 110
Hilary of Poitiers, St., 146
Hill, Edmund, 173
Hirsch, Eric Donald, 33, 161
Hitler, Adolf, 5, 117
Holdcroft, David, ix
Holman, Susan R., 162
Homer, 2, 164, 168
Hooker, Morna D., 87–88, 168
Hughes, Gerard W., 26, 160
Hull, F. C., 159
Hunt, Holman, 166

Ignatius Loyola, St., *passim*
Innocent III, Pope, 130
Iparraguirre, Ignacio, 176
Irenaeus of Lyons, St., 114
Isabella I of Castile, Queen, 128
Ivens, Michael, 176

Jacobi, J., 159
Jacopone da Todi, 106
James, Clive, 161
James of Voragine, 6, 127
Jerome, St., 83, 147–48, 173
John Chrysostom, St., 127
John of the Cross, St., 147,
    152, 173
John Paul II, Pope St., 45, 47,
    151
Joseph, St., 63–66, 70, 165
Joseph of Arimathea, 7, 109
Juan II of Castile, King, 128
Judas Iscariot, 45, 97, 107–11,
    142, 162
Jung, Carl Gustav, 4, 159
Justin Martyr, St., 66, 114

Kant, Immanuel, 40, 162
Kendall, Daniel, 160, 170, 176
Keylock, Leslie Robert, 167
Kierkegaard, Søren, 60–61, 163
Kolvenbach, Peter-Hans, 171
Krailsheimer, A. J., 171
Krause, Deborah, 89–90, 168–69

LaBelle, Jeffrey, 160, 170, 176
Langland, William, 126, 171
Langton, Cardinal Stephen, 130
Larkin, Philip, 11
Leclercq, Jean, 147, 173
Leonard, Richard, 26, 160
Leonard of Port Maurice,
    St., 113
Levine, Amy-Jill, 168
Liebert, Elizabeth, 176
Lock, Elizabeth, ix
Lombard, Peter, 30
Lonergan, Bernard, 144

Loughnane, Michael, ix
Louis of France, St., 92
Louth, Andrew, 161, 173
Lowrie, Walter, 163
Lucifer, 7, 18, 20, 39, 54, 78, 80, 88, 126, 156
Ludolph of Saxony, 7, 8, 127, 157, 159
Luther, Martin, 69, 165
Luz, Ulrich, x

MacMillan, Sir James, 115
Magi, The, 62, 64, 131
Mahoney, Jack, 171
Mao Zedong, 117
Marcus, Joel, x, 88, 168
Marshall, D. G., 161
Martin, James J., 176
Martin, Ralph, 162
Martini, Cardinal Carlo Maria, 145, 152
Mary Magdalene, St., 84, 127, 130–32, 139, 172
Masaccio, 46
Merrigan, Terrence, 164
Metz, Johannes Baptist, 79, 166
Metzger, Bruce M., 170
Michelangelo, 93
Miller, Susan, 84, 166–67, 169
Misrahi, Catherine, 173
Molin, J.- B., 33, 161
Moloney, Francis J., 86–88
Moses, 2, 21, 28, 94–96, 108, 111
Mülhaupt, Erwin, 165
Munitiz, Joseph A., viii, ix, 159–61, 163–64, 166, 171, 176
Mutembe, P., 32–33, 161

Nau, Pascale Dominique, 173
Newman, St. John Henry, 2, 3, 5
Newsom, Carol A., 167
Nicodemus, 97
Nineham, Dennis, 83–86, 166–67

Oden, Thomas C., 163
O'Leary, Brian, 170
O'Reilly, Terence, 176
Origen, 66, 73, 146–48, 150, 152, 173
Otto, Rudolf, 28, 160
Owen, Wilfrid, 115

Palestrina, Giovanni Pierluigi, 115
Pascal, Blaise, 117, 171
Paulin-Campbell, Annemarie, 176
Paul the Apostle, St., 2, 4, 17–18, 57–58, 61, 85, 88–89, 99, 135, 137, 147, 168, 172, 178
Paul III, Pope, 160, 163
Pellauer, David, 161
Pesch, Rudolf, 169
Peter the Apostle, St., passim
Piero della Francesca, 166
Pilate, Pontius, 108–10, 162
Plato, 37
Poitier, Sydney, 135
Pol Pot, 117
Pseudo-Bonaventura, 127
Pseudo-Dionysius the Areopagite, 136

Rahner, Karl, 112, 144
Raphael, Melissa, 160

Rejadell, Teresa, 129
Rembrandt, 108, 166
Richard of Chichester, St., 58
Richard of St. Victor, 144
Ricoeur, Paul, 33, 161
Ringe, Sharon H., 167
Roemer, Judith A., 176
Rogier van der Weyden, 128
Romanos the Singer, St., 127
Roosevelt, Eleanor, 2
Roser, Isabel, 166
Rouault, Georges, 166
Rousse, Jacques, 173
Rupnik, Marko, 114

Sallman, Warner, 166
Sarah, wife of Abraham, 2,
    12, 28
Satan. *See* Lucifer
Schemel, George J., 176
Schmalz, Timothy, 116–17
Schottroff, Luise, 89
Schweizer, Eduard, 169
Scotus, Blessed Duns, 39
Searle, Mark, 30–31, 33, 161
Seneca, 95
Shakespeare, William, 20
Shea, John, 170
Sheldrake, Philip, 176
Shepherds near Bethlehem,
    The, 62, 64, 67–69,
    71, 76
Siebenrock, Roman A., 164
Smit, Peter-Ben, 169
Smith, Michael, ix
Socrates, 17, 37
Stalin, Joseph, 117
Steiger, Rod, 135
Stein, Robert H., 169

Stevenson, Kenneth W., 30–31,
    33, 171
Strauss, Mark L., 169
Studzinski, Raymund, 172, 173

Tanner, Norman P., 174
Tatian, 127
Tavener, Sir John, 115
Taylor, Vincent, 169
Tellechea Idígoras, José
    Ignacio, 177
Teresa of Kolkata, St. Mother,
    2, 3
Tertullian, 45
Tetlow, Joseph A., 177
Theonas of Alexandria, St.,
    145–46, 173
Thérèse of Lisieux, St., 174
Thomas à Kempis, 8
Thompson, J. B., 161
Tolbert, Mary Ann, 89, 167
Tolkien, J. R. R., 131
Toner, Jules J., 177
Trotter, William F., 171
Trouvé, Marianne Lorraine, 174
Tyndale, William, 64, 70

Van der Weyden, Roger, 128
Venantius Fortunatus, St., 163
Vermeersch, Arthur, 56–57, 163
Victoria, Tomás Luis de, 115
Virgil, 2
Vona, Costantino, 171

Wallace, Daniel B., 167–68
Walsh, Brendan, ix
Walsh, James, ix, 173
Walsh, Milton, 7, 151
Watts, Isaac, 116

Weinsheimer, J., 161
Wesley, John, 2–4
Wicks, Jared, ix, 148–51,
    173–74
Willcock, Christopher, ix
Williams, Monty, 177
Wipo of Burgundy, 163

Wood, Allen W., 162
Wren, Brian, 82

Xavier, St. Francis, 43

Zurbarán, Francisco de, 116

BIBLICAL INDEX

OLD TESTAMENT

Genesis

3:12–13	47
3:21	48
4:15	48
4:23–24	47
6:1–4	47
18:1–15	28

Exodus

2:23–4:17	28
3:1–6	21
3:14	108, 111
20:21	21

2 Samuel

11:1–27	48

Psalms

16:9	129
16:11	129
19:1	94
22	20, 119
34:8	63
110	53
131:2	153
139	20
145–50	17

Song of Songs

8:6–7	144

Isaiah

1:3	66
60:1–5	94

Micah

5:2–5a	74

Jonah

3:4	45

NEW TESTAMENT

Matthew

1:3	83
1:20	130
1:20–24	20
1:23	153
2:10	131
3:13–17	82
4:16	130
5:1–12	157
5:35	53
5:45	144
6:19–21	79
8:5	131
8:5–10	137

8:14–15	83	1:41	86, 87, 168, 169
8:20	99	2:1	87
9:9	92	2:1–12	87
9:9–13	93	2:9	85
11:20–24	137	2:11	85
11:24–30	156	2:18–20	84
12:30	156	3:1–6	87
13:24–30	156	3:3	85
21:15	137	3:10	87
22:14	162	3:31–35	84
25:31–46	48	4:3–9	136
25:41	45	5:21–43	84
26:24	45	5:24–34	87
26:53	108	5:25–34	86
27:3–5	109, 162	5:27–31	87
27:6–10	162	5:41	85, 87
27:7–10	109	5:41–42	88
27:19	109	6:3	84
27:24	109, 162	6:5	87
27:61	130	6:14	85
27:62–66	130	6:14–29	84
28:1	130	6:16	85
28:2–7	20	6:51	132
28:4	130	6:56	87
28:5–10	130	7:24–30	84, 87
28:8	131	7:32–33	87
28:9	131	8:22–25	87
28:10	131	9:2–8	96
28:11–15	130	9:6	96
28:17	131	9:14–29	87
28:20	82, 153	9:26–27	85
		9:29	16
Mark		10:17–22	12
1:12–13	37, 84	10:28	109
1:13	88, 152	10:35	85
1:18–19	90	10:35–45	85
1:29	85	10:41	85
1:29–31	83, 86, 90, 169	10:43	85
1:31	89, 152, 169	10:45	84, 85, 88, 152

10:46–52	87	2:11	110
10:49	85	2:12	69
10:52	167	2:13–14	67, 69
12:26	85, 88	2:14	69
12:41–44	84	2:15	68
14:3–9	84, 91, 169	2:16	69
14:10–11	108	2:19	76
14:14	71	4:38–39	83
14:21	108	5:1–11	28
14:28	85	7:13	74
14:42	108	8:2–3	137
14:44	108	8:4–15	72
14:50–52	109	9:11–17	72
14:52	109	9:12	70
14:66–69	84	9:28–36	94
15:1	108	10:1–12	39
15:10	108	10:13–15	137
15:15	108	10:18	39
15:21	170	10:25–37	48, 70
15:39	96, 108, 109, 137	10:29	73
15:40–41	88, 109	10:29–37	72
15:40—16:8	84, 87	10:33	74
15:41	86, 89, 90, 152, 169	10:34	67, 71
15:42–47	109	11:29	48
15:47	109	12:16–21	46
16:1–8	131	12:35–38	46
16:6	85, 90, 168	13:15	66
16:7	90	15:3–7	72
16:8	132	15:11–24	43
		15:11–32	48, 96, 135
Luke		15:15–17	37
1:5	83	15:17	48
1:26–38	57	15:20	135
1:35	130	15:22–23	135
2:1–5	64	15:23	129
2:7	65, 67, 69, 71	15:24	129
2:8–9	69	15:32	129
2:8–20	68	16:19–31	48, 165
2:10	69	18:10–14	165

19:1–10	75	3:16	135
19:5	75	5:1–18	96
19:7	70, 75	6	141
22:7–13	75	6:1	141
22:8–12	71	6:1–15	140
22:11	67, 71, 75	6:8–11	140
22:12	75	6:11	140
22:15–20	76	6:25–71	142
22:19	76	6:27	140
22:43–44	114, 170	6:35	140
22:48	110	6:44	29, 140
22:51	110	6:51	111, 140
22:61	110	6:67–68	141
22:62	38	7:37–39	144
23:6–12	110	8:31–38	12
23:27	109	9:1–41	97, 139
23:27–31	110	9:5	139
23:34	110	9:7b–34	97
23:39–43	109	10:10	140
23:43	110	10:11	74
23:49	110	10:14	74
23:53	66	11:1–45	96
24:4	69	12:1–11	142
24:26	56	12:4–8	142
24:36	69	12:32	140
24:50–52	132	13:21–30	142
24:52	69	13:31—17:26	129
		14:1	129
John		15:15	129
1:4	140	18:1–11	110
1:4–9	110, 140	18:5	111
1:38	29, 111, 141	18:5–8	108
1:42	141	18:9	111
1:43	141	18:18	110, 142
2:3–4	142	19:25–27	128
2:4	141	19:31–37	113
2:11	139	20:8	144

20:11–18	139, 172	8:4	58
20:19–23	60, 130, 139	8:11	58
20:24–29	139	8:38–39	80
21	139, 141–43, 172	12:2	18
21:1	141	15:25	85
21:1–2	139		

1 Corinthians

21:2	139	1:18–23	99
21:4	139	2:7	18
21:6	140	2:20	18
21:7	139, 144	4:16	58
21:8	140	9:5	166
21:9	140, 141	11:1–2	58
21:10	140	13:1–13	58
21:11	140	13:4–8a	135, 172
21:12	139		

2 Corinthians

21:13	140	3:3	168
21:14	172	6:4	168
21:15–17	141	8:9	99
21:15–19	143	11:8	168
21:18–19	141	11:23	168
21:19	141	13:5	17
21:20	142		

Galatians

21:22	141	4:4	57
		5:13	58

Acts of the Apostles

Ephesians

1:1–12	132	1:18	12, 144
1:14	128, 130	6:12	20
3:1	165		

Philippians

3:11	165	1:9	138
4:3	165	1:9–10	18
4:19	165	2:8–11	61
8:14	165	3:8	148, 149
19:22	85	3:10	58
		3:21	58

Romans

6:1–11	58
6:1–23	89
6:3–4	89

Colossians

3:16   151

1 Thessalonians

1:6   58

2 Thessalonians

3:7   58

1 John

1:2–3   150

2:2   18

2:16   18

Revelation

17:14   53

21:1–4   95